SWEETWATER

James Vickery

SWEETWATER

Copyright © 2012 by James Vickery

Published by: Theocentric Publishing Group
               1069 Main Street
               Chipley, Florida 32428

               http://www.theocentricpublishing.com

All rights reserved. No part of this book may be reproduced or transmitted in any form or by any means without written permission of the author.

Unless otherwise noted Scripture is taken from the New King James Version. Copyright © 1979, 1980, 1982 by Thomas Nelson, Inc. Used by permission. All rights reserved.

Library of Congress Control Number: 2012935359

ISBN 9780983244189

FOR

My sweet and loving wife

Cynthia Ann Vickery

Foreword

God saved the Israelites from slavery in Egypt and promised them a land flowing with milk and honey. A short time after the miraculous escape the people complained because the water at Marah was bitter. Moses cried out to God and the waters were made sweet.

The bitter springs forth from the sinful nature. The sweet springs forth from the well of God's goodness, mercy, and grace. Christians may experience some bitterness in this life. However, God can turn bitter water into sweet water.

This book is a summary of how the bitter is made sweet by the grace of God. Jesus Christ suffered the bitterness of human life so that Christians could experience the sweetness of divine life. You may face suffering, sickness, emotional distress and many other bitter experiences, but God is able to make the bitter water turn into sweet water.

Table of Contents

1. God Makes Life Sweet 1
2. Edge of a Promise 9
3. The Modern Myth 17
4. The Faith Way 27
5. Dignity of Humility 37
6. Life of Prayer 45
7. Special Relationships 55
8. The Most Wanted 63
9. A Heavy Load 69
10. Spiritual Patriotism 75
11. Secure Investments 83
12. True Religion 93
13. Marks of a Christian 101
14. Christian Love 116
15. Encouragement is Sweet 123
16. Sweet is the Word 131

1. God Makes Life Sweet

So Moses brought Israel from the Red Sea; then they went out into the Wilderness of Shur. And they went three days in the wilderness and found no water. Now when they came to Marah, they could not drink the waters of Marah, for they were bitter. Therefore the name of it was called Marah. And the people complained against Moses, saying, "What shall we drink?" So he cried out to the LORD, and the LORD showed him a tree. When he cast it into the waters, the waters were made sweet. There He made a statute and an ordinance for them, and there He tested them, and said, "If you diligently heed the voice of the LORD your God and do what is right in His sight, give ear to His commandments and keep all His statutes, I will put none of the diseases on you which I have brought on the Egyptians. For I am the LORD who heals you." Then they came to Elim, where there were twelve wells of water and seventy palm trees; so they camped there by the waters.

Exodus 15:22-27

John and Rascas decided to go down to the Sweetwater spring for a refreshing drink of cool spring water. John was the youngest and Rascas enjoyed playing tricks on John. It was late summer. The old persimmon tree along the path was loaded with fruit that was just getting ripe. Persimmons are very bitter until they are fully ripe. As they walked along the path, Rascas thought of a trick to play. "John, have you ever eaten a persimmon?" John didn't know what a persimmon was, much less tasted one. "Oh, you missed out on the sweetest fruit," Rascas said trying to allure the young lad. "Look, I can reach a persimmon," Rascas said stretching his body to reach one on a lower limb. With the persimmon in hand Rascas said, "Take a big bite to get the full flavor!" John grabbed the persimmon and took a big bite. The bitterness stunned John but like the eruption of volcano, he egested the bitter persimmon. Rascas laughed as John's contorted facial expression was that of anger. Rascas tried to save face by urging John to hurry to the Sweetwater to get some relief. The cool refreshing spring water washed away the bitterness of the persimmon.

The only way to overcome a bitter experience in life is to experience the sweet taste of pure goodness. Children are taught to pray, "God is great, God is good, let us thank Him for this food." The sad commentary to that little prayer is that the children are not taught the meaning of greatness and goodness relative to God. Christians ought to desire an understanding of God's goodness in contrast to man's badness. The bad news is the badness of sin that makes life bitter. The good news is the goodness of God makes life sweet. A brief review of King David's life and King Solomon's life in Israel will help us understand. David and Solomon trusted and worshipped God, but they were also notorious sinners. God announced His kingdom covenant to David. Solomon was God's instrument to establish the Temple in Jerusalem. After the Temple was dedicated Solomon sent the people of Israel to their homes, "joyful and glad of heart for the good that the Lord had done for David, for Solomon, and for His people Israel" (2 Chronicles 7:10). The bitterness of sin plagued David, Solomon, and the people of Israel, but it was the goodness of God that produced the sweet life of joy and gladness of heart. Sin makes life bitter, but God makes life sweet.

Two Greek words will help us understand the meaning of good relative to God. They are agathos and kalos. Agathos translated "good", generally describes something that is good and useful, especially the moral goodness of God. Kalos translated good, refers to that which is beautiful and noble. The Greek ideal was to pursue the good and the beautiful in life. In contrast to evil is good. One is bitter and one is sweet. In contrast to ugly is the beautiful. One expresses the appearance of bitterness and the other expresses the appearance of goodness.

Mark's account of the gospel of Christ has an interesting twist to the theory of "good". A prominent man in the community went to Jesus and said, "Good Teacher, what shall I do that I may inherit eternal life?" Of course, the man did not know he was speaking to the second person of the trinity. Jesus did not give him the Roman road or the three steps to salvation. Jesus did respond to the man with a rhetorical question. One question deserves another so Jesus said, "Why do you call Me good? No one is good but One, that is, God" (Mark 10 17-18). Then Jesus quotes several of the commandments. Clearly, in this context, the word good, agathos, refers to moral goodness. Since man is a sinner, moral goodness will never be pure in this life. It is a fundamental principle of the Christian religion that bitterness will be part of the human experience. God alone is morally pure; therefore, God alone is the ultimate good.

It will be easier to understand "good" in everyday life if we briefly examine the development of Christianity in the Western world. Until the advent of the American and French revolutions, Christians aspired to understand and live according to the good. In Augustine's treatise on the *Nature of Good*, he said, "The highest good, than which there is no higher, is God..." (*Nature of Good*, chapter 1). Augustine goes on to declare the truth that has been trampled under foot in contemporary Christianity. He said, "That all good things are from God alone, suffices for their correction, if they were willing to give heed, as I said above. Not, therefore, are great good things from one, and small good things from another; but good things great and small are from the supremely good alone, which is God" (*Nature of Good*, chap. 12). Tracing the development of the "goodness" doctrine through Medieval Christianity, we find the men like Thomas Aquinas boldly declaring that God is the good of all good. To put it another way God is the highest Good. Then as today, people tend to follow the teaching of cultural elites such as universities, business executives, therapeutic advisors, politicians, and the arts and media sub-culture. They say "everything is good."

A cultural shift began to take place in the 18th century when the cultural elites switched from the good to the happy. "Life, liberty, and the pursuit of happiness" became the model for which Americans were very "happy" to include into their worldview. The French switched from the good to the happy with "liberty, equality, and fraternity". Who wants to pursue God's goodness when one can have human happiness?

In his book, *Kingdom Triangle*, Philosopher J. P. Moreland, illustrates the modern dilemma. "Under the influence of naturalist and postmodern ideas, many people no longer believe that there is any ultimate meaning in life that can be known. These folks – and they are legion – have given up on seeking that meaning and instead are living for happiness. Today, the good life is a life of happiness, and it is the goal most people have set for themselves and their children. A major talk radio host has interviewed hundreds of people over the last few years by asking the question, 'What did your parents want most for you – success, wealth, to be a good person, or happiness?' Eighty-five percent said 'happiness.'" The evidence is abundant that the general public, and sadly Christians, have set the goal in life to experience human happiness even if it means forgetting God's goodness" (*Kingdom Triangle*, J. P. Moreland, page 23).

The passion for happiness is not something new. The inspired story of God freeing the Israelites from slavery is eye opening. After a miraculous release, the Israelites found themselves standing before the Red Sea. Their confidence in the goodness of God was shattered by a trial in the wilderness. Then they said to Moses, "Because there were no graves in Egypt, have you taken us away to die in the wilderness? Why have you so dealt with us, to bring us up out of Egypt? Is this not the word that we told you in Egypt, saying, 'Let us alone that we may serve the Egyptians'? For it would have been better for us to serve the Egyptians than that we should die in the wilderness" (Exodus 14:11-12). It is a mistake to measure God's goodness by the volume of His generosity. However, God miraculously opened the Red Sea and the Israelites crossed over without any loss of life. God was and is good. On another occasion, the Israelites found themselves unhappy with the goodness of God. The children of Israel expressed their unhappiness to Moses and Aaron saying, "Oh, that we had died by the hand of the LORD in the land of Egypt, when we sat by the pots of meat and when we ate bread to the full! For you have brought us out into this wilderness to kill this whole assembly with hunger" (Exodus 16:3). How quickly they – we – forget the goodness of God. J. P. Moreland explains what happens when

Christians forget the goodness of God. "If you spend all your time trying to be happy, you end up focusing all your attention on yourself and how "happy" you are and, as a result, you become a shriveled self who can't live for some larger cause. Your life will center on yourself and your moment-by-moment focus will be on how you feel inside. Your sole criterion of evaluation for seeking a job, making friends, finding a spouse (or staying with a spouse!), and selecting a church will reduce to one overarching concern: How does this particular thing make me feel? The best way to be happy in the contemporary sense is to forget about it, to try to live a good life for a bigger purpose, especially for the cause of Christ" (*Kingdom Triangle*, J. P. Moreland, page 24).

"A bigger purpose" in life is to go beyond your appetite to glorify and exalt pleasure and sensual happiness. Set your goal to do all things for the glory of God. The benediction in the book of Hebrews announces the blessing that reveals the light of God's glory. "Now may the God of peace who brought up our Lord Jesus from the dead, that great Shepherd of the sheep, through the blood of the everlasting covenant, make you complete in every good work to do His will, working in you what is well pleasing in His sight, through Jesus Christ, to whom be glory forever and ever. Amen" (Hebrews 13:20-21).

"A bigger purpose" in this life is to enjoy the Creator and His creation. The Psalmist explains that "it is good for me to draw near to God; I have put my trust in the Lord GOD, That I may declare all Your works" (Psalm 73:28). To enjoy God means that you experience a unique relationship with Him. You are also able to enjoy God's creation. God makes life sweeter by His presence with you and His presents to you.

Although the bitterness of sin brings disorder, it is well to remember that God is in control. God is sovereign which means that He has ultimate power and authority. He "works all things according to the counsel of His will" (Ephesians 1:11). What does "the counsel of His will" mean? Does that mean that God got together with the other two parties in the Godhead to collaborate with them? Does it mean that God is unsure of Himself and His purpose? The answer is no, no, no! Here "the counsel of His will" refers to God's purpose in the destiny of all things, which God determines without reference to any outside source. God makes life sweeter by having everything under His generous and loving care.

God has already made life sweeter by providing eternal salvation to His people through His only son, the Lord Jesus Christ; "for He will save His people from their sins" (Matthew 1:21). The Lord Jesus not only saved His people, He is the Mediator between God and man. As a prophet, he gave His people the Word of God, which speaks to His people as fresh as the morning newspaper. As a Priest, he has made the ultimate sacrifice to satisfy the wrath the Father had against His people. As a King, the Lord Jesus Christ rules over His people. God made life sweeter by sending His son to save His people.

God will continue to make life sweeter by the power of the Holy Spirit. Jesus said, "And I will pray the Father, and He will give you another Helper, that He may abide with you forever" (John 14:16). The Holy Spirit enables you to believe that God will make your life sweeter.

Trying to find pleasure in food, drink, possessions, good health, long life or any desire to make the body happy is a waste of time. Trying to live a happy life will finally cause restlessness and unfulfilled desires. True pleasure and happiness belong to the soul. Engagement in some human activity does not produce true pleasure and happiness. Glorify God and there is true pleasure. Enjoy God and there is true happiness. Do not eat a bitter persimmon when you have the sweet honey of God's love.

2. Edge of a Promise

These are the words which Moses spoke to all Israel on this side of the Jordan in the wilderness, in the plain opposite Suph, between Paran, Tophel, Laban, Hazeroth, and Dizahab. It is eleven days' journey from Horeb by way of Mount Seir to Kadesh Barnea. Now it came to pass in the fortieth year, in the eleventh month, on the first day of the month, that Moses spoke to the children of Israel according to all that the LORD had given him as commandments to them, after he had killed Sihon king of the Amorites, who dwelt in Heshbon, and Og king of Bashan, who dwelt at Ashtaroth in Edrei. On this side of the Jordan in the land of Moab, Moses began to explain this law, saying, "The LORD our God spoke to us in Horeb, saying: 'You have dwelt long enough at this mountain. Turn and take your journey, and go to the mountains of the Amorites, to all the neighboring places in the plain, in the mountains and in the lowland, in the South and on the seacoast, to the land of the Canaanites and to Lebanon, as far as the great river, the River Euphrates. See, I have set the land before you; go in and possess the land which the LORD swore to your fathers—to Abraham, Isaac, and Jacob—to give to them and their descendants after them.'

Deuteronomy 1:1-8

John and his family lived in upstate New York during the middle of the nineteen century. John received word from a friend in California informing John of the Gold Rush. John's friend even sent him a map that virtually promised a vain of Gold. It was located in the green valley near Yellow creek. John died before he could make arrangements to move. John passed the map along to his son, Joe, and urged him to go west. Joe eventually took his

Dad's advice and moved to California. He found a valley next to the green valley, but decided to settle there because of the alleged threats of danger near Yellow creek. He lived his whole life digging for gold that was, as promised, just a few miles away.

How many people live on the edge of a promise? The Bible furnishes abundant evidence that God's people have, at various times, lived on the edge of a promise. A brief survey of the Israelites release from Egyptian bondage until they settled in the land of Canaan demonstrates how God's people lived on the edge of a promise.

> Now they departed and came back to Moses and Aaron and all the congregation of the children of Israel in the Wilderness of Paran, at Kadesh; they brought back word to them and to all the congregation, and showed them the fruit of the land. Then they told him, and said: "We went to the land where you sent us. It truly flows with milk and honey, and this is its fruit. Nevertheless the people who dwell in the land are strong; the cities are fortified and very large; moreover we saw the descendants of Anak there. The Amalekites dwell in the land of the South; the Hittites, the Jebusites, and the Amorites dwell in the mountains; and the Canaanites dwell by the sea and along the banks of the Jordan." Then Caleb quieted the people before Moses, and said, "Let us go up at once and take possession, for we are well able to overcome it." But the men who had gone up with him said, "We are not able to go up against the people, for they are stronger than we." And they gave the children of Israel a bad report of the land which they had spied out, saying, "The land through which we have gone as spies is a land that devours its inhabitants, and all the people whom we saw in it are men of great stature. There we saw the giants (the descendants of Anak came from the giants); and

we were like grasshoppers in our own sight, and so we were in their sight" (Numbers 13:26-33).

God promised Abraham "the land of Canaan as an everlasting possession" (Genesis 17:8). God promised Moses to bring His people to the "land of the Canaanites…to a land flowing with milk and honey" (Exodus 3:17).

God brought His people to the edge of the promise. They rebelled and refused to believe God's promise and obey Him. Later Moses reminded the children of Israel of their rebellion. " Thus your fathers did when I sent them away from Kadesh Barnea to see the land. For when they went up to the Valley of Eshcol and saw the land, they discouraged the heart of the children of Israel, so that they did not go into the land which the LORD had given them" (Numbers 32:8-9).

These verses remind us of God's covenant plan, which are the promises of God for the people of God. The Lord had already given them the land. Their duty was to believe God's covenant promise and move into the land. God's relationship with His people is by way of covenant.

The whole Bible consists of God making covenants with His people. For instance, the Bible begins with God making a covenant with Adam. God made a covenant with Noah. This covenant pattern continues throughout Scripture. God not only made covenants with big names like Adam, Noah, Abraham, Moses and so forth, He made covenants with all His people, rich, poor, educated, and uneducated. For instance he made a covenant with the nation of Israel to "obey the voice of the Lord your God, to keep His commandments and His statutes which are written in the book of the Law" (Deuteronomy 30:10). God also made a promise to save those who confess and believe the gospel of Jesus Christ and His saving grace (Romans 10:9).

When God makes a covenant he makes a promise, but there are stipulations that require a response from His people. In Deuteronomy thirty the stipulation is obedience and devotion to God. In Romans ten the stipulations are confession and faith. If you believe and obey, there is a blessing. If you do not, there will be unpleasant circumstances.

Man being the sinner he is, he breaks God's covenant. God then keeps his promise to bring about the consequences of breaking the covenant. This covenant process naturally leads to a broken relationship between holy God and sinful man. So is there any hope for those who profess true faith, yet break God's covenant. Yes the hope is in God's promise of salvation through Jesus Christ the covenant keeper.

Christ kept the covenant that Adam could not keep which means Christ kept the covenant for all those whom God calls to Himself. (See Romans 5:12-19).

God gave His people freedom from slavery in Egypt; He guided them to the edge of the land flowing with milk and honey. Then the covenant people of God rebelled and broke covenant with God. The result was unfavorable. "According to the number of days which you spied out the land, forty days, for every day you shall bear your guilt a year, even forty years, and you shall know My opposition. 'I, the Lord, have spoken, surely this I will do to all this evil congregation who are gathered together against Me. In this wilderness they shall be destroyed, and there they shall die.' "

(Numbers 14:34-35) Then for nearly 40 years they wandered around in no man's land suffering the consequences of their sin.

After forty years they found themselves on the edge of a promise. When they arrived on the east side of the Jordan in the land of Moab, it was a crucial moment for God's people.

They had lived on the edge of a promise too long. God reminded them of His promise. "See, I have set the land before you; go in and possess the land which the Lord swore to your fathers – to Abraham, Isaac, and Jacob – to give to them and their descendants after them." (Deut 1:8).

There are two conflicting views relative to the interpretation of this text. One is that the present location of the Israelites on the East Side of the Jordan in Moab represents the secular world. The land, which the Lord swore to give to the people of Israel, the Promised Land it is called, represents the sacred world. It is the new heavens and the new earth.

Another view is that the Promised Land is this present world, but God's people must have dominion over it. When the whole earth has been subjected to Christ the King, then God will establish the new heavens and the new earth.

It doesn't matter which view you take, all agree that there are two dimensions involved in the Christian life: the "already" and the "not yet" or the present time and the time to come.

Christians are called to live in the tension between the present time and the time to come.

There is a sense in which we all live on the edge of a promise in this secular world. The fulfillment of the promise is in the sacred world to come.

When we walk the streets of life we should seize the moment. In the face of danger, find the courage to live by these words which Moses spoke to all Israel. When God commissions you to turn and take your journey don't fear the moment, but rather seize the moment. Sometimes men are afraid to execute what God has entrusted to them, just as the Israelites had done 40 years before they returned to the edge of the Promised Land.

The work God gives you to do today should be done today whether it is in the land of Moab or in the land of promise. If we live in the tension between the present time and the time to come we will escape two extremes. The one extreme is that this present time is all that counts. The other extreme is the time to come is all that counts. Jesus says we are to be salt and light in this present time. The cultural mandate found in Genesis one should ever be before us. We have the duty to exercise dominion, but the mandate and the duty should never become our god.

God has given each of His children an inheritance. If you belong to Jesus Christ, you have an inheritance. It may be small or it may be large. It is a promise from a covenant making sovereign God. It is up to you to enlarge it. Turn and take your journey and go in and possess it. God's promise to you is not on the edge. It is in the inheritance.

It has the promise of grace and God's blessing to a wayward church living in this postmodern world. Have you thought about entering into the land of truth?

Maybe we would all do well to enlarge upon the first few words of Deuteronomy: "There are the words." They will take us into the land of truth. When you go into the land of truth you are entering a large land, but God has promised to give it to you. With that truth turn and take your journey and go in and posses the land in which you live, work, go to school, and every civil institution.

Now I grant that the land is large. Moses tells us it is in the plain, the mountains, in the lowland, in the South, (no mention of the north) and on the seacoast. No matter how big and how difficult the job, we need to remember that God said "I swore to give to them" and God will keep His promise

Which generation are we? Are we going to remain in Moab or will we turn and take our journey? Because of their rebellion and false worship, it took the Israelites forty years to do what should have taken eleven days.

If you live on the edge of God's promise, return to the Lord. The only remedy for rebellion against God's promises is to return to the Lord. God reminds His people to get off the edge and come into the land of promise.

Deuteronomy 30:2 - Return to the LORD your God and obey His voice, according to all that I command you today, you and your children, with all your heart and with all your soul,

2 Chronicles 30:9 - For if you return to the LORD, your brethren and your children will be treated with compassion by those who lead them captive, so that they may come back to this land; for the LORD your God is gracious and merciful, and will not turn His face from you if you return to Him."

Isaiah 31:6-7 - Return to Him against whom the children of Israel have deeply revolted. For in that day every man shall throw away his idols of silver and his idols of gold—sin, which your own hands have made for yourselves.

Hosea 14:1 - O Israel, return to the LORD your God, for you have stumbled because of your iniquity; Take words with you, And return to the LORD. Say to Him, " Take away all iniquity; Receive us graciously, For we will offer the sacrifices of our lips.

Joel 2:13 - So rend your heart, and not your garments; Return to the LORD your God, For He is gracious and merciful, Slow to anger, and of great kindness; And He relents from doing harm.

Zechariah 1:3 - Therefore say to them, 'Thus says the LORD of hosts: "Return to Me," says the LORD of hosts, "and I will return to you," says the LORD of hosts.

Those words are as fresh today as they were over twenty five hundred years ago; "return to the Lord with words." Return with words of confession, asking forgiveness and for the grace of repentance. Above all, return to the Lord with a thankful heart that you are able to believe His promises.

Moses was the covenant mediator for Israel. Jesus Christ is your Mediator. Listen to His stipulations in the Word of God and return to the Lord.

3. The Modern Myth

My brethren, count it all joy when you fall into various trials, knowing that the testing of your faith produces patience. But let patience have its perfect work, that you may be perfect and complete, lacking nothing. If any of you lacks wisdom, let him ask of God, who gives to all liberally and without reproach, and it will be given to him. But let him ask in faith, with no doubting, for he who doubts is like a wave of the sea driven and tossed by the wind. For let not that man suppose that he will receive anything from the Lord; he is a double-minded man, unstable in all his ways. Let the lowly brother glory in his exaltation, but the rich in his humiliation, because as a flower of the field he will pass away. For no sooner has the sun risen with a burning heat than it withers the grass; its flower falls, and its beautiful appearance perishes. So the rich man also will fade away in his pursuits. Blessed is the man who endures temptation; for when he has been approved, he will receive the crown of life which the Lord has promised to those who love Him. Let no one say when he is tempted, "I am tempted by God"; for God cannot be tempted by evil, nor does He Himself tempt anyone. But each one is tempted when he is drawn away by his own desires and enticed. Then, when desire has conceived, it gives birth to sin; and sin, when it is full-grown, brings forth death.

James 1:2-15

The power company just turned off the electricity for your town. There was no more phone service. All automobiles were confiscated and every convenience in life disappeared. Everyone wonders how he or she will survive without a cell phone! They will not be able to walk around the grocery store texting. How true, because there are no more grocery stores. Is this the end of the world? No, it is 33 A.D. in Jerusalem. It was a time when life was uncluttered with gadgets and a luxurious lifestyle. Today being without a phone or an automobile is a test of one's character. A Christian might say it was a trial or a test to endure.

The modern Christian myth is that Christians will not have to endure the trials of life. How many times have we heard these words, "Come to Jesus and all your problems are over." Health problems will disappear. Wealth will appear. If you do have trials, self-esteem will be the victor. How could a Christian have trials in life if God loves him or her; God has a wonderful plan that does not include suffering and trials

Jesus faced trials, testing, and temptation all the way to the cross. Peter wrote the early church and reminded them that they had been "grieved by various trials" (1 Peter 1:6). The Lord Jesus Christ said Paul "must suffer for My name's sake" (Acts 9:16). The apostle Paul suffered "a thorn in the flesh" (2 Corinthians 12:7). The Lord warns his followers that they would be persecuted (John 15:20). The Bible ought to purge the Christian mind of the modern myth that the Christian life is all hunky-dory. Christians will "fall into various trials" (James 1:2).

Although some Christian leaders avoid teaching this text, it is actually good for Christians to be aware of the reality of trials. Even if the Bible did not explicitly state that Christians would face trials, temptations, suffering and persecution, the doctrine of sin is the source of all of them.

The Book of James is an excellent resource to study for a better understanding of the trails and temptations that Christians meet with each day. The inspired Word of God makes a bold statement against the modern myth that good health, wealth, and happiness are the abiding companions for the Christian life. Sometimes it is referred to as prosperity theology. The bold biblical statement is, "My brethren, count it all joy when you fall into various trials" (James 1:2). Notice the terminology, "My brethren" is plural and refers to all Christians. It is a statement of fact that Christians will face trials. It is not if you face trials, it is when you face trials. God sends trials to the Christian, because He is a sovereign and loving God.

The stated purpose of the trial is "the testing of your faith." The Lord Jesus Christ suffered death. Paul suffered labors, imprisonments, beaten, often in danger of death, stoned, and shipwrecked. Christians suffer and some Christians seem to have suffered more than others.

Church history reveals an abundance of suffering for each generation. The average Christian in the United States is virtually empty of knowledge relative to the history of the church. Little is known of the suffering and persecution of our ancestors. However, the church on trial was strong and experienced the Sweetwater effect of God's spring of hope.

Christians experience various kinds of trials. The more serious the trial the more tested is the faith. Dr. Adoniram Judson was the first missionary to Burma. He faced trials in this life that most people only read about in books. He devoted most of his adult life serving on the mission field in Burma. He translated the whole Bible into the Burmese language. He worked six years before there was one convert to Christianity. Later thousands would come to Christ. His life was also a life of trials. He suffered imprisonment, disease and health problems, hunger, cruelty, and the loss of his wife ands children, and then loneliness. For Adoniram Judson, the testing of faith, ended when he went home to be with the Lord.

The death of a loved one, disease, sickness, divorce, and rebellious children are a few examples of trials that touch the Christian life. There are other small trials such as having a flat tire on the way to work or someone criticizing your work.

Sometimes trials come without warning, when they are least expected, but rarely what appears to us as a convenient time. When trials come your way, accept them humbly realizing that God will bring good out of the trial. Christians often react to trials with ill-advised zeal or to the other extreme with fear.

Christians must consider it all joy when they encounter various trials. The trials of life do not necessarily bring joy, but the believer must meet them with joy. It is all about trust God's sovereignty and that God has not made a mistake.

How often do trials come and the response is "blessed be the name of the Lord." That is exactly what Job said, "The Lord gave and the Lord has taken away. Blessed be the name of the Lord" (Job 1:21).

Since the trials of life are often hard to understand, the only ultimate source that will give relief is from God. Go to God in prayer and commit the trials to your heavenly Father.

Trials are part of the learning process for Christians. You will be able to determine your level of faith, when you encounter trials. Whether you are rich or poor, you will learn the depth of your faith. The rich may have faith in their earthly wealth. The poor may have displaced faith in someone or the ability to overcome his or her situation. The trials of life always teach us just how much we trust God. Whether we are rich or poor, we must treat trials with joy, and ask God for wisdom.

The Bible says, "the testing of your faith produces patience" (James 1:3). Christians benefit from trials that produce endurance in this life. The word patience refers to Christian steadfastness and Christian perseverance. It is a patient endurance.

Trials produce a positive result; they help us see the beauty of the two sisters called grace and mercy. Trials also prove our love to Christ. Then Christ grants to us the crown of life. Christ said, "Do not fear what you are about to suffer....Be faithful until death, and I will give you the crown of life" (Revelation 2:10). Trials are life giving and needed for Christian growth and maturity.

Your life is full of trials and those trials are truly blessings. Jesus ended the lessons of the nature of a Christian with these awesome words. "Blessed are those who are persecuted for righteousness' sake, For theirs is the kingdom of heaven. Blessed are you when they revile and persecute you, and say all kinds of evil against you falsely for My sake. Rejoice and be exceedingly glad, for great is your reward in heaven, for so they persecuted the prophets who were before you" (Matthew 5:10-12).

Although the trials you endure for the sake of Jesus Christ have a great reward, sometimes trials turn into temptations. What appears to be a trial may actually be a temptation. Jesus said, "Watch and pray lest you enter into temptation" (Matt 26:41).

Suppose someone close to me was diagnosed with a terminal disease. This would certainly be a trial, but it could become a temptation. If I questioned God's goodness and mercy, then temptation has taken control.

The point is a trial can easily become a temptation. Lot's wife faced a real trial in Sodom. She didn't want to leave the city. Lot, his wife and children were told, "not to look behind you" but Lot's wife "looked back behind him, and she became a pillar of salt" (Genesis 19:17-26). Lot's wife let the trial turn into a temptation. The result was disastrous. We all face trials that can become temptations.

God sends trials but Satan does the tempting. The temptations began with Eve in the garden of Eden and will not end until the Lord Jesus Christ returns.

Christians must identify the source of temptation. "Let no one say when he is tempted, 'I am tempted by God'; for God cannot be tempted by evil, nor does He Himself tempt anyone. 14 But each one is tempted when he is drawn away by his own desires and enticed" (James 1:13-14).

The Bible makes it clear that the source of temptation is not God. It has become very popular even among evangelical Christians to say, "I'm a victim." The therapeutic industry promotes victimizationalism. The cry is "I'm a victim" of abuse, mistreatment, circumstances, and the list goes on. The victim mentality has been popularized because the church in the western world has trampled under foot the doctrine of sin. There is a tendency in man to blame others for his own sin. For instance, in the garden of Eden, God instructed Adam to tend and keep the garden. Eve was tempted by the serpent and she allowed the temptation to turn into sin. God questioned Adam about the sin, and Adam blamed Eve, the woman that God gave Adam. Eve blamed the Serpent. To sin is bad enough, but to blame it on someone else is worse. The victim mentality is to blame others when temptation overcomes and turns into sin.

The source of temptation cannot be God, "for God cannot be tempted by evil, nor does He Himself tempt anyone." The source of temptation is from the sin nature of man because "each one is tempted when he is drawn away by his own desires and enticed." Temptation comes from "his own desires", not the desires of someone else; not the desires of Satan. The Bible emphasizes individual responsibility.

Christians ought to spend more time reflecting on the nature of sin and less time reflecting on self worth. The sin nature and the actual sins ought not to overcome the believer, because God's grace is all about forgiveness.

God allows Christians to face trials for their own good, but God also enables Christians to deal with the trials of life. However, the sin nature is inclined to rebel against God. The sin nature nurtures the temptations that turn into actual sins. Guard against the desire of the heart because "The heart is deceitful above all things, and desperately wicked" (Jeremiah 17:9).

The desire may seem irresistible, but God will provide a way. The Bible explains that "No temptation has overtaken you except such as is common to man; but God is faithful, who will not allow you to be tempted beyond what you are able, but with the temptation will also make the way of escape, that you may be able to bear it" (1Corinthians 10:13).

The Bible explains the progression of trials and temptations. "Then, when desire has conceived, it gives birth to sin; and sin, when it is full-grown, brings forth death" (James 1:15).

Death is not merely a biological function that terminates physical activity such as many atheists teach. Christians believe that death is the end of physical life as we know it, but death is not the end of a relationship with God. Every human being has a soul that will remain eternally, in a favorable relationship with God or an unfavorable relationship with God. If the guilt of sin is not removed and the actual sins are not forgiven, then death will seal an eternal unfavorable relationship with God. The first step for living with trials and resisting temptation is to be in a right relationship with God. The next step is humble yourself before God asking forgiveness of the actual sins committed.

God is the giver of good gifts, but we are so busy opening the bad gifts, we overlook the good gifts. "Every good gift and every perfect gift is from above, and comes down from the Father of lights, with whom there is no variation or shadow of turning" (James 1:17). God gives sinners new hearts so they are able to believe the gospel of Jesus Christ. God forgives sins. God adopts the believing and forgiven child into the family of God. Then God gives the strength to live with trials and live with temptations. God is the giver of the greatest gifts.

Although God is the giver of all good gifts, he does not give his child a license to live like an animal. Christians have certain responsibilities as they live with trials and resist temptation. "So then, my beloved brethren, let every man be swift to hear, slow to speak, slow to wrath; for the wrath of man does not produce the righteousness of God" (James 1:19-20).

God expects us to keep our mouths shut and our ears open. We are not able to hear the wisdom of God, found in the Word of God, unless God is the focus of our attention. We must also resist outbursts and fits of anger. The word anger or angry is a condition of the mind and expression of human emotions. It is about as hard to define as the word love. Then there are those who equate anger with contemptuousness and contentiousness. Contemptuousness refers to an arrogant and defiant person. Contentiousness refers to hostility and strife. Anger is a biblical concept associated with that dimension of the soul called the affections in previous centuries, but now generally referred to as the emotions. Any expression of the emotions may be sinful or it may be righteous. The only way that sinful men, and all men are sinful, may interpret an emotional concept is to understand the biblical teaching of that particular concept, whether it is love, anger, or hate. Although anger for the glory of God is not sinful, anger often overrules the grace of God.

If Christians do not face trials, then something may be wrong. "all who desire to live godly in Christ Jesus will suffer persecution" (2 Timothy 3:12). Any kind of persecution is a trial. If trials are turning into temptations on a regular basis, you probably need to consult the training manual (the Word of God). If temptations turn into evil actions on a regular basis, you should ask the question: "Am I truly God's child and have I experienced His forgiveness?" If the answer is yes then all the trials and temptations aggravate you, but they will not control you.

Trials and temptations may be like bitter water. It may taste horrible and may even make you sick. Go to God through the Lord Jesus Christ by the power of the Holy Spirit and you will find Sweetwater.

4. The Faith Way

I say to you, I have not found such great faith, not even in Israel.

Luke 7:9

Augustine of Hippo said, "Faith is not belief without proof, but trust without reservation." Faith is difficult to define in modern English because faith is used like butter. It is spread wide but shallow, it quickly melts, and under heat, it becomes unstable. An ocean of ink has been used over the past two thousand years to explain meaning and application of faith to the human experience.

Faith is a word used often in the Bible, more often in the New Testament than the Old Testament. It is wise to trace the word faith as much as possible to its root. The root will produce many branches and leaves, but the root is the foundation for the tree. The root of faith begins with intelligent consciousness. The ability to believe is an expression of that intelligent consciousness. Faith or belief follows persuasion. Faith (belief) requires an object. For example, I believe that automobile insurance is necessary in our modern world. The object of my belief (faith) is in automobile insurance. First, I had to have enough intelligence to form the words into a sentence. Then I had to have some knowledge of automobile insurance and why it is a good investment. Finally, I have to trust the company that promises to pay in the event of a loss. Take those principles and apply them to man in his relationship to God and you have the fundamental principles of biblical faith. The gospel of Luke tells the story of a man with remarkable faith.

> Now when He concluded all His sayings in the hearing of the people, He entered Capernaum. And a certain centurion's servant, who was dear to him, was sick and ready to die. So when he heard about Jesus, he sent elders of the Jews to Him, pleading with Him to come and heal his servant. And when they came to Jesus, they begged Him earnestly, saying that the one for whom He should do this was deserving, "for he loves our nation, and has built us a synagogue." Then Jesus went with them. And when He was already not far from the house, the centurion sent friends to Him, saying to Him, "Lord, do not trouble Yourself, for I am not worthy that You should enter under my roof. Therefore I did not even think myself worthy to come to You. But say the word, and my servant will be healed. For I also am a man placed under authority, having soldiers under me. And I say to one, 'Go,' and he goes; and to another, 'Come,' and he comes; and to my servant, 'Do this,' and he does it." When Jesus heard these things, He marveled at him, and turned around and said to the crowd that followed Him, "I say to you, I have not found such great faith, not even in Israel!" And those who were sent, returning to the house, found the servant well who had been sick. (Luke 7:1-10)

The warnings about hypocrisy from the previous text must be taken into account as we look at the text in chapter seven. When Jesus used the word hypocrite, most of the time he was directly addressing Pharisees and scribes. They were the Jewish religious leaders during the earthly ministry of Jesus. They were to the Old Testament what professing believers are in the New Testament. Jesus used the word hypocrite to describe those Jewish religious leaders who were wicked and crafty, although they professed to believe the Word of God.

Hypocrisy is not just a 1st century phenomena, it has plagued the church throughout its history. Hypocrisy kills Christianity because it reflects a bad image of the Christian religion. A hypocrite puts on a false face. The hypocrite deliberately acts outwardly religious, but inwardly they are profane and godless.

Jesus denounced the hypocrites as unfaithful men. In the context of this hypocrisy, Luke records the account of Jesus making a comparison of the unfaithful hypocrite to a faithful sinner. There is false confidence of the hypocrite's profession of faith.

It was the Jewish elders, the hypocrites opposed to ministry of Jesus that made an appeal to Jesus to save the life of the centurion's slave. It was the Jewish elders, hypocrites according to the mouth of Jesus, who hated the ministry of Jesus, but loved their ways and tradition. These hypocrites, and all hypocrites, have a false hope because they overestimate human worth.

The Jewish elders told Jesus, "He is worthy" referring to the worth of the Centurion; the equivalent of an Army Captain leading approximately 100 men. The word "worthy" refers to something having merit, value, dignity, and character. A false view of human worth in relation to God's worth is often associated with a false view of faith.

The Jewish elders had a false view of human beings because of the false worth in the object of their worship, the Centurion. They said the Centurion was worthy because he loved the Jewish nation. Apparently, their view of reality was distorted because the Jewish nation didn't even exist, except in their minds.

A false view of human worth plagues the church. Many hypocrites believe their church deserves attention and honor above others. To say that one church is more worthy than another church is unbiblical. There is a true faithful church and there is a false unfaithful church.

The Jewish elders said, "He (the Centurion) loves our nation." Perhaps the Centurion respected the shadow of monotheism that he saw in the Jewish religion. That does not make him any more or less worthy than any other Gentile inclined toward the Jewish religion.

Another obvious reason for the Jewish elders' faith in the Centurion was that he built the Jewish synagogue.

Hypocrites deceive themselves by their own false hope. In contrast to the false faith of the hypocrite is the true certainty of the sinner's faith.

It all begins with the intelligent consciousness of the Centurion. "Lord I am not worthy for you to come under my roof" (Luke 7:6). The Centurion recognized, intelligently, of his unworthiness compared to worthiness of Jesus Christ. The Centurion knew that Jesus was a Jew and apparently, he didn't want to ask Jesus to break the time-honored custom that a Jew must not enter a Gentile home. The Centurion not only felt insufficient to ask Jesus into his home, the Centurion was filled with a sense of personal unworthiness. The Centurion saw his insignificance in comparison to the significance of Jesus Christ.

The Centurion was a sinner. He was aware that there was no merit in his benevolence to the Jews when he compared himself to dignity, majesty, and love of Jesus Christ.

This Centurion possessed the grace of God, which the hypocrites despised and rejected. The hypocrite is filled with pride and works righteousness, while the sinner saved by grace is filled with brokenness and humility. One is without true faith and the other is full of faith.

The faith of the hypocrite and the faith of the sinner will be measured to him in relation to his need before God. Great faith comes from a great need. Israel was self-righteous; they did not need faith. The Jewish elders did not confess and acknowledge their unworthiness; they had faith in their perceived worthiness.

The Centurion's servant was healed. Whose faith healed the servant? The question is wrong because "faith" does not have the power of creation, thus the power to create a healthy body. However, Jesus said of the Centurion, "not even in Israel have I found such great faith." Obviously, the Centurion had faith, but what was the object of his faith? The Bible gives the answer. The Centurion confessed his unworthiness and then said to Jesus, "just say the word, and my servant will be healed." The Centurion had an intelligent consciousness of who Jesus was. He had knowledge of the power of Jesus and he trusted Jesus, who alone had the power to create or restore the servant's health.

It is God's grace that enables one to believe; then the believer will demonstrate his or her faith. Ask Jesus Christ to give you the power to believe and practice the Christian religion.

The apostle's asked Jesus to "Increase our faith" (Luke 17:5). This request came after an extended ministry with the Lord Jesus Christ. They had seen the miraculous power of Jesus Christ. It was evident that Jesus was God in the flesh. The Disciples of

Christ confessed their faith in Christ on several occasions. One notable confession of faith was by Peter in Caesarea Philippi.

The ministry of Jesus in Caesarea Philippi with his disciples was a time for Jesus to teach his disciples without the interference he might have expected from the Jews and Herodians in Galilee and Jerusalem.

Jesus had two important questions for the disciples. What did the people in general think about Jesus and what did the disciples think about Jesus.

The answer that fell from the lips of Peter was "Thou art the Christ, the Son of the living God" (Matthew 16:18) Peter had already made several impromptu declarations about Christ. In Luke chapter five, Peter confessed that Jesus was the Lord. In John chapter six Peter said, "We have come to believe and know that You are the Christ, the Son of the living God" (John 6:69).

You might not think Peter's confession was so significant since millions have since confessed that Jesus is the Christ, the Son of the living God. Yet Peter made his confession of faith when the rulers of Israel were opposed to Jesus. Peter made his confession when he saw Jesus in the form of a servant. Peter believed (had faith) when it was unpopular and even dangerous to confess that Jesus was the promised Messiah.

Peter's confession of faith was indeed one of the first and in many ways a unique creed of the Christian church. A creed is a statement of one's belief. The English word creed comes from the Latin word credo, which means, "I believe." Every rational human being believes, because it is impossible to live in this life without believing something. Knowledge of the object of faith is necessary to believe.

Peter's faith was based on his belief and knowledge that Christ was the Son of the living God

God enables Christians to believe. During Paul's missionary journey to Philippi, he met a woman that experienced a change in her life.

"And on the Sabbath day we went outside the gate to a riverside, where we were supposing that there would be a place of prayer; and we sat down and began speaking to the women who had assembled. And a certain woman named Lydia, from the city of Thyatira, a seller of purple fabrics, a worshiper of God, was listening; and the Lord opened her heart to respond to the things spoken by Paul" (Acts 16:13-14).

The power of the Holy Spirit renewed her mind. God the Holy Spirit enabled her to believe the truth of the Word of God. The Holy Spirit of God also changes the will so that the truth of the Word of God can be acted upon. After God changes the heart, the converted sinner will then believe the Word of God, even if it seems unbelievable.

Faith is necessary to trust God and His Word. Christians enjoy faith because they love the truth found in the love and grace of God. Faith is necessary for fellowship with the Savior. Faith is necessary for all spiritual relationships. Therefore, faith is an activity of the whole soul.

If you believe, then you must have faith, and if you have faith, you must have knowledge. It is impossible to assert any truth if utter ignorance prevails.

There is an old maxim attributed to Saint Hilary of the fifth century. "A person cannot express what he does not know and he cannot believe what he cannot express." Hilary's words agree with the words of our Lord in the gospel of John. Jesus said: "If I do not do the works of My Father, do not believe Me; but if I do them, though you do not believe Me, believe the works, that you may know and understand that the Father is in Me, and I in the Father" (John 10:37-38). The Lord did not say believe without providing a reason to believe.

Jesus persuaded the disciples by His works to prove that He was the Son of God. What was the means of persuasion? It was evidence, such as Jesus reversing the course of nature or healing a terminally ill person, or more significantly raising someone from the dead.

It has been said that faith does not require being convinced or persuaded. I'll let the Bible speak for itself. And as Jesus passed on from there, two blind men followed Him, crying out, and saying, "Have mercy on us, Son of David!" And after He had come into the house, the blind men came up to Him, and Jesus said to them, "Do you believe that I am able to do this?" They said to Him, "Yes, Lord." Then He touched their eyes, saying, "Be it done to you according to your faith" (Matthew 9:27-29).

The blind men certainly believed – they had faith – but it was because they were convinced that Jesus was the Son the David, the Messiah who had the power to heal.

True faith is not found in false securities that torment professing Christians with doubts and wavering. Firm faith is true faith. The apostle John says is best: "These things I have written to you who believe in the name of the Son of God, in order that you may know that you have eternal life."

The sweetest faith in the world believes that Christ suffered and died for the sake of _____ and fill in your name. If you truly do not believe that, ask God to give you faith as he gave to Peter, "Thou art the Christ, the Son of the living God."

If you have already believed for the salvation of your soul then I commend to you these words:

"Beloved, while I was making every effort to write you about our common salvation, I felt the necessity to write to you appealing that you contend earnestly for the faith which was once for all delivered to the saints." (Jude 1:3).

5. Dignity of Humility

It is doubtless not profitable for me to boast. I will come to visions and revelations of the Lord: I know a man in Christ who fourteen years ago—whether in the body I do not know, or whether out of the body I do not know, God knows—such a one was caught up to the third heaven. And I know such a man—whether in the body or out of the body I do not know, God knows— how he was caught up into Paradise and heard inexpressible words, which it is not lawful for a man to utter. Of such a one I will boast; yet of myself I will not boast, except in my infirmities. For though I might desire to boast, I will not be a fool; for I will speak the truth. But I refrain, lest anyone should think of me above what he sees me to be or hears from me. And lest I should be exalted above measure by the abundance of the revelations, a thorn in the flesh was given to me, a messenger of Satan to buffet me, lest I be exalted above measure. Concerning this thing I pleaded with the Lord three times that it might depart from me. And He said to me, "My grace is sufficient for you, for My strength is made perfect in weakness." Therefore most gladly I will rather boast in my infirmities, that the power of Christ may rest upon me. Therefore I take pleasure in infirmities, in reproaches, in needs, in persecutions, in distresses, for Christ's sake. For when I am weak, then I am strong. I have become a fool in boasting; you have compelled me. For I ought to have been commended by you; for in nothing was I behind the most eminent apostles, though I am nothing. Truly the signs of an apostle were accomplished among you with all perseverance, in signs and wonders and mighty deeds. For what is it in which you were inferior to other churches, except that I myself was not burdensome to you? Forgive me this wrong!

2 Cor. 12:1-10

Booker T. Washington once said: "No race can prosper till it learns that there is as much dignity in tilling a field as in writing a poem." It appears that Booker T. Washington thought that dignity has its place in the personality rather than position. Dignity belongs to the character of a personality. Dignity is demonstrated by respect for the proper order of creation and excellence in life.

I rarely hear the word dignity used and when it is used it has a connection to power and authority which implies position. For instance, the head of a state may be referred to as a dignitary. Dignity refers to the worthiness of a person, not the worth of the position in life.

As a word, dignity appears only a few times in the Bible. In the New Testament it is associated with leadership in the church. It has an ethical and aesthetic dimension referring to the order and reverence for godliness.

Christians must think of dignity in the right sense, because human dignity and divine dignity must be distinguished. The dignity of God denotes the majestic, holy, reverence due Him in all His perfections. His noble unsearchable mind, His perfect wisdom, His impeccable judgment and His benevolent character reflect God's dignity. The dignity of man is fallible and filled with all sorts of confusion.

We cannot discuss the dignity of man without discussing two factors that shape our understanding of dignity. These two factors are self-image and identity.

On one extreme a person may view him or herself as worthless and not worthy of the next breath. The other extreme is one feels so full of self-importance that he or she thinks they have become a god to be worshipped. I've known people in both categories. Those who think they are worthy of worship are the ones that are most visible. Christians must avoid both categories. I believe the apostle Paul teaches us to balance our dignity with humility.

Jesus was fully human, but His sinlessness gives the perfect example of simplicity and versatility. His suffering and power, His humility and dignity are worthy of our attention. Although we are sinners and unable to express the perfection of these attributes, we still ought to hold them as our goal in life.

In the early 1980's R. C. Sproul wrote a book entitled *In Search of Dignity*. There is, according to Sproul, an "aspiration for significance," a "quest for esteem" deeply imbedded within the human person. I believe that Dr. Sproul is right, but I also believe that sin is deeply imbedded within the human person, so how does man understand his worth? Sproul's answer was, "Man's dignity rests in God who assigns an inestimable worth to every person."

It is not up to us to determine our worth. It is up to us to understand our worth. The only way we can do that is to have a balanced understanding of ourselves according to Scripture. Therefore all Christians must understand dignity and humility from a biblical perspective. The apostle Paul understood that humility and dignity are gifts from the Lord.

Paul's opponents at Corinth were true blue boasters. Paul was embarrassed by the occasion. He didn't want to boast, but he had to defend his apostleship. He understood the dignity that God had assigned to him, but he also understood the humility that marked his service to the Lord.

Humility is not a characteristic that describes a weakly, soft-spoken, lowly person. On the contrary, humility is a quality that reflects the relationship of a submissive servant serving a worthy master. Moses was the most humble man on earth, but his walk with the Lord and his leadership ability reflects his dignity. For Christians dignity is demonstrated by believing God's word reflected by their godly actions. Not sinless actions, but godly actions.

According to the Word of God, Paul was honored above all the apostles. The Bible says Paul was caught up to the third heaven and caught up into Paradise. This language has entertained many a person with its metaphysical implications. The metaphysical is beyond human sensations, but Paul indicates he experienced something beyond this physical world. He even said he heard "inexpressible words".

I will not speculate about the third heaven or paradise. I will say that they are parallel terms. I simply mean there are two ways of describing the same thing. It was a typical Hebrew literary technique known as parallelism. Let me give you an illustration of parallelism in the Old Testament.

The **law of the Lord** is **perfect**
The **testimony of the Lord** is **sure**
The **statutes of the Lord** are **right**
The **commandment of the Lord** is **pure**
(Psalm 19)

The law, testimony, statutes, and commandment are parallel terms. However, they all refer to the Word of God. Likewise, the third heaven and paradise mean the same thing. Where is this third heaven and what happens there?

Paul does not say. In fact, Paul is so careful that he describes this event in the third person. He doesn't want to get involved in the explanation and description of the place he calls paradise. Paul was bodily raptured into heaven as was Enoch and Elijah. The only difference is that Paul returned with a knowledge of heaven.

I want to point out that the death experience of Paul is not accompanied with a story of what it is like in heaven. A few Christians claim to have died and had a metaphysical experience accompanied by bright lights, the senses exhilarated, and beautiful scenes. Jesus raised Lazarus from the dead, but the Word of God never mentions Lazarus boasting about his visit to heaven, paradise or the third heaven. We should all ask ourselves this question: Why does the only infallible record (the Bible) not mention what happens in the death experience, but sinful men are quick to say that they had visions after the physical body was terminated?

Paul's purpose for mentioning his experience was not to brag about his rare human experience, but to get the message across to the duped Corinthians. What was Paul's message? Simply that Paul had more dignity than all the fake teachers and deceitful workers put together.

Paul could say "I am a dignitary". At the same time Paul shows the Corinthian Church that there is no dignity among the false teachers and deceitful workers.

There is a lesson here for the proud and arrogant who think they are above others in position or rank in life. God will eventually bring down the proud and arrogant. Jeremiah the prophet said, "Behold I am against you O arrogant one delcares the Lord God of hosts for your day has come, The time when I shall punish you and the arrogant one will stumble and fall with no one to raise him up." (Jeremiah 50:31ff) "The proud looks of man shall be humbled, The haughtiness of men shall be bowed down And the Lord alone shall be exalted" (Isaiah 2:11).Malachi likewise said, "For behold the day is coming, Burning like an oven, and all the proud, yes, all who do wickedly will be stubble. (Malachi 4:1) The Corinthians had fallen into the sin of arrogance and pride. Paul reminded them, "you have become arrogant, and have not mourned instead, in order that the one who had done this deed might be removed from your midst." (1 Corinthians 5:1).

It should be observed from Scripture that the Lord punishes the proud and arrogant, but the Lord rescues the humble. The prophet Zephaniah said, "I will leave in your midst a meek and humble people, and they shall trust in the name of the Lord." (Zephaniah 3:12) If you expect the Lord to find favor in man-made dignity, you are in for a surprise. The Lord shows favor to the humble that trust in His name.

God created man in His image which means that humans have great intrinsic value. However sin has defaced human dignity. Sinful man wants to be God. Sinful man sees dignity as the ultimate attribute and he sees humility as a shameful attribute.

The Lord Jesus was humble and He taught humility. He made it plain that "whoever exalts himself will be humbled, and he who humbles himself will be exalted" (Luke 14:11). Boasting and bragging is sinful. When I hear a professing Christian boasting and bragging on some achievement or another, I wonder if they realize what they're doing.

The apostle Paul had an abundance of extra ordinary revelations which entitled him to a place of honor above the rest, but to protect him and literally to protect his very soul the Lord gave Paul a thorn in the flesh. We don't know what the thorn was except that it is a figure of speech that described a real physical problem that the Apostle Paul had to endure. What we do know is that Paul's opponents were critical of his weaknesses, some of which may very well have been a result of the thorn in the flesh. The Bible indicates that a messenger of Satan tormented Paul. Satan tormented Job and expect it may have been a similar experience for Paul.

In Paul's case we know that he found relief in God's grace. So can you! God resists the proud, but gives grace to the humble. Paul's only boast was in his weaknesses and his strength was from Christ. The Lord said "My strength is made perfect in weakness.

In a nutshell, Paul's dignity rested in his humility. Paul has set up a model for elders in the church. Dignity is the standard for church elders in both doctrine and life. They are to rule their own families well and lead an honorable life in the community. The redemptive work of Christ applied to His people will bring dignity to His humble people.

6. Life of Prayer

Brethren, my heart's desire and prayer to God for Israel is that they may be saved. For I bear them witness that they have a zeal for God, but not according to knowledge. For they being ignorant of God's righteousness, and seeking to establish their own righteousness, have not submitted to the righteousness of God. For Christ is the end of the law for righteousness to everyone who believes. For Moses writes about the righteousness which is of the law, "The man who does those things shall live by them." But the righteousness of faith speaks in this way, "Do not say in your heart, 'Who will ascend into heaven?'" (that is, to bring Christ down from above) or, "'Who will descend into the abyss?'" (that is, to bring Christ up from the dead). But what does it say? "The word is near you, in your mouth and in your heart" (that is, the word of faith which we preach): that if you confess with your mouth the Lord Jesus and believe in your heart that God has raised Him from the dead, you will be saved. For with the heart one believes unto righteousness, and with the mouth confession is made unto salvation. For the Scripture says, "Whoever believes on Him will not be put to shame." For there is no distinction between Jew and Greek, for the same Lord over all is rich to all who call upon Him. For "whoever calls on the name of the LORD shall be saved.

Romans 10: 1-15

Paul was an evangelist and preacher, but he was also a pastor. As a pastor he loved the church of God. You can't love the church without loving the people in the church.

I hope you are not deceived by the use of the word love. It is not a word that merely describes an emotional response one person has for another. Love has the best interest of the loved at heart. True love touches the whole soul, the mind, the will and the emotions.

Paul loved the church even though it had members who acted very un-Christian. Paul also loved those outside the church, even those who despised the gospel.

When a pastor watches people violate the Word of God and they seek to establish their own righteousness and salvation, it can be very painful. The pastor knows that he has no power to save the soul of that individual that God has put under his care. The pastor certainly knows he has no power to save the soul of someone outside the fellowship of the church.

So what did pastor Paul do even though he concluded that all human beings, are in need of God's saving grace. What does the pastor do when he knows they are hopeless without the righteousness of Christ?

He prays for their salvation. The Apostle Paul was a man of prayer. He made prayer a regular part of his world and life view. Paul believed that prayer should be intelligent, consistent, and continual.

All Christian ministry ought to begin with prayer. After God saves a sinner, the first desire is to evangelize others. Unfortunately the excited young Christian forgets the first step. Evangelism begins with prayer. Most evangelicals today suppose that man can be converted by following a certain plan or by devising a method that will cause someone to accept Christ. Such ideas are not taught in Scripture. However, Scripture does teach us that we must have a passion for the salvation of the lost and pray for their salvation. Pray we must, but our prayers must be preceded by a passion for the lost.

All of our prayers are in vain if we are not in a right relationship with God. "If I regard iniquity in my heart, the Lord will not hear" (Psalm 66:18).

We all know that Romans is the great theological book in the Bible. The doctrines of original sin, regeneration, justification, adoption, and sanctification are carefully outlined, not to mention the unheard doctrine in the church such as predestination and election. Even so the Bible uses those words often. Many people believe that election and predestination are barriers to evangelism.

Paul certainly didn't think so. Predestination is no barrier to evangelism. In fact, Predestination by a sovereign God ought to be the stimulating factor to pray for the salvation of those whom God has called to himself. Our attitude toward men is not to be governed by God's secret counsel concerning them.

We must be like the Apostle Paul. We must have as our "heart's desire" the salvation of lost sinners. If the "heart's desire" is to save the lost then by all means save them. If the "heart's desire" is to obey God, then pray that God will save the lost.

Your passion to pray for the lost sinner will increase as you understand the sovereignty of God. Even if we arouse all our passions and pray for the lost, we must direct our prayers to the God who provides salvation for the lost. God not only provides salvation, He is our salvation. When the Ark of the Lord was returned to Jerusalem after the Philistines were defeated, David said in his prayer of thanksgiving "Save us, O God of our salvation. . . (1 Chronicles 16:35).

When David prayed his prayer of repentance he said "Deliver me from the guilt of bloodshed, O God, The God of my salvation. . . . (Psalm 51:14). Over and over again the Bible uses the same language - The God of my salvation.

The Bible is abundantly clear that God declares some people righteous according to the righteousness of Christ. The Bible is abundantly clear that God sanctifies some for His good pleasure. And the Bible is abundantly clear that God will glorify some for His own glory. If the Bible abundantly and clearly explains the doctrine of salvation, then salvation is something that God the Father, God the Son, and God the Holy Spirit does for His own glory. If our salvation is from God, then we must pray to Him for salvation.

I am convinced that if we would run away from man-made methods of evangelism and return to biblical standards, we would see the saving grace of God working in the lives of men, women and children.

It is not just the duty of the pastor to offer up prayers for salvation, it is the duty of all Christians to pray for the salvation of sinners. Prayer for the salvation of the lost is specifically a duty for all God's children. Paul told the Thessalonian church - and by extension and application - he speaks to all the church in all ages that they must pray always. Paul said "pray without ceasing" because prayer is the will of God in Christ (1 Thess. 5:17). Paul called the saints at the church at Rome - brethren. It was Paul's way of calling the whole church to this noble work. It is a reflection of Paul's charged emotions and affection for those who are without the righteousness of Christ, whether in the church or out of the church. Paul's spiritual patriotism is reflected by "his heart's desire and prayer to God" for his fellow countrymen.

The highest good you can hope for your loved one or friend is the salvation of his or her soul. And even more so for your enemy. The best thing that could ever happen to your enemy is to be converted to the Christian religion. He or she would no longer be your enemy, but a brother or sister. This unique relationship brings unity to the church. (See Philippians 2:2).

Now you might ask how should you pray for the salvation of a lost soul? Pray that God would open their eyes to the righteousness of Christ. Of course they cannot see the righteousness of Christ until they see their sinful condition. So pray that they will see their depraved nature and that God will save them in spite of their depravity.

Pray that they would stop seeking to establish their own righteousness and their ignorance of God's holiness and righteousness will be removed. Pray that they will confess with their mouth that Jesus Christ is Lord and believe in their heart that God has raised Him from the dead. Pray that God would send a preacher and that the preacher will preach the gospel of peace. Pray that God will send a teacher that will teach the full counsel of God.

Dr. B. B. Warfield left us with these words that describes the hope of praying Christians. "Redeemed by Christ, regenerated by the Holy Spirit, justified through faith, received into the very household of God as His sons, led by the Spirit into the flowering and fruiting activities of the new life, our salvation is still only in process and not yet complete. We still are the prey of temptation; we still fall into sin; we still suffer sickness, sorrow, death itself....When Christ comes... there shall be a new heaven and new earth, in which dwells righteousness."

Praying for the salvation of sinners is not enough. Christians are commanded to pray for saved sinners. "Now I pray to God that you do no evil, not that we should appear approved, but that you should do what is honorable, though we may seem disqualified. For we can do nothing against the truth, but for the truth. For we are glad when we are weak and you are strong. And this also we pray, that you may be made complete" (2 Corinthians 13:7-9).

Pastor's have the uncomfortable responsibility for saved sinners. It is an awesome responsibility because the Bible says Pastor's will be held accountable. The metaphors in Ezekiel would probably frieghten a person that does not understand God's grace and forgiveness. God says things like, and I'll paraphrase, Ezekiel, representing pastor's, if you don't warn the people of their sins, you will die. It's really not a pleasant thought so that is apparently the reason pastor's rarely preach on Ezekiel chapter thirty three.

Psychology has radically affected the pastoral ministry over the last century, to the degree that many churches now almost exclusively focus on the therapeutic model. Many pastors are using man made psychological methods to help sinners maintain some sanity. They resort to man made managerial theories to keep the saved sinner for jumping ship.

Our Lord expects pastors to feed the flock, not with man-made inventions, but with the Word of God. The Holy Spirit and the Word of God are God-made for sinners.

Religious programs will not cause saved sinners to have a sense of security that they have a right relationship with God through Jesus Christ by the power of the Holy Spirit. Sunday school, small group meetings, youth programs, weight loss programs and a dozen other programs are not biblical mandates for strengthening the souls of men. All these are recent inventions of the liberal church and the shift to a social gospel. Sunday school may be useful to learn more about a religious subject. Small group meetings may bring Christians together for fellowship. Youth programs may attract young people to participate in church activities. A weight loss program may strengthen your body, but it will not strengthen your soul. It is the Spirit of God that enables you to understand God's Word by the power of the Holy Spirit which is the source of your strength.

Paul said the pastor has the primary responsibility for equipping the saints for the work of ministry (Eph 4:12)

The standard has been set by the Word of God, but that doesn't always mean that pastors will be faithful to the Word of God. Sometimes men have falsely perceived that God called them to pastor God's people, when in fact they should be working as a car salesman, a politician, or some other trade in which they can use their silver tongue.

However, some pastors are in their proper place exercising God's gift of preaching, exhortation, teaching, evangelizing and serving faithfully by example. They are following biblical principles in their quest to equip the saints for the work of ministry.

You would think that doing all the right things would bring pastoral success to the church. That is not so. Next to the Lord Jesus Christ, the apostle Paul was probably the most gifted pastor in all the Christian church. As a pastor, the apostle Paul devoted his life to the task of equipping the saints for ministry. Many of the churches that Paul started were messed up within a few years and some of them had serious problems.

Sanctification is the word that describes the process of growing up in Christ and endeavor, let me say it again, endeavor to turn away from sin. The agent of sanctification is the Holy Spirit, but God uses means or instruments in the process of sanctification.

The Word of God is the primary means or the primary instrument of our sanctification. It is the pastor's job to explain the Word of God to the congregation, so they will be equipped for works of ministry and therefore grow in their sanctification.

What happens when the pastor does his job, but the congregation doesn't grow in their sanctification? He does the same thing the Apostle Paul did - He prays - He prays for their sanctification. Paul prayed for the sanctification of the church members in Corinth, because he knew God alone could renew their hearts, minds, wills and affections thus enabling them to grow spiritually.

Paul knew that the problems at Corinth were horrible. The problems at Corinth would make any pastor go to his knees. Listen to some of the problems at the Corinthian church:

1 Cor. 1:10 - "Now I plead with you, brethren, by the name of our Lord Jesus Christ, that you all speak the same thing and that there be no divisions among you. . . .

1 Cor. 3:3 - "For where there are envy, strife, and divisions among you, are you not carnal and behaving like mere men?

1 Cor. 4:18 - "Now some of you are puffed up (arrogant)."

1 Cor. 5:1 - "It is actually reported that there is sexual immorality among you. . . ."

1 Cor. 6:1 - "Dare any of you, having a matter against another, go to law before the unrighteous and now before the saints?"

1 Cor. 6:9-11 - "Do you not know that the unrighteous will not inherit the kingdom of God? Do not be deceived. Neither fornicators, nor idolaters, nor adulterers, nor homosexuals, nor sodomites, nor thieves, nor covetous, nor drunkards, nor revilers, nor extor-

tioners will inherit the kingdom of God. And such were some of you. . . ."

1 Cor. 11:18 - "For first of all, when you come together as a church, I hear that there are divisions among you. . .."

With so many problems in the church you might think the great Apostle would throw up his hands and say "I give up" but Paul didn't give up.

He worked and he prayed; Paul prayed that the congregation would be enabled to die unto sin and live unto righteousness.

Paul prayed that they "may be made complete" (2 Corinithains 13:9). Paul does not have Christian perfectionism in mind. The word complete comes from the Greek word katartizw. Jesus used the word referring to those who are "fully trained." When an unskilled worker is trained he is reformed in his thinking and practice. The word was originally used to refer to putting something in a proper condition.

Paul prayed that the Corinthian church would be made complete or we might say the prayer was that they would be reformed in their thinking and practice. The Corinthian church was in need of reformation and restoration. They needed to repair what had been broken. They needed to repair the division, strife, envy, arrogance, and immoral behavior that had put their spiritual growth on hold. Their sanctification was in reverse.

Paul's prayer for the congregation at Corinth included a negative command (a "do not" command) and a positive command (a "do" command).

First his prayer is that they would do no evil. This command is necessary for all Christian believers to progress in their sanctification.

Second his prayer is that they should do what it honorable. The word "honorable" is rarely used this day and age. It comes from the Greek word kalos which refers to the good and the beautiful. When it applies to ones character it takes the form of virtue and excellence.

Paul's prayer is that they would seek harmony and union rather than separation and division. That they would seek peace and concord rather than strife and disagreement. That they would show compassion and benevolence rather than envy and jealousy. That they would replace arrogance with humility and immoral behavior with decent moral behavior.

True harmony, peace, benevolence, and humility is a mark of spiritual growth. Those are the things that the congregation at Corinth needed to do to repair the broken relationships with each other - with their pastor, the apostle Paul and ultimately with God Himself.

When we pray for sanctification of the members of the church, we are praying for the reformation of the church. We are praying that its members will turn from sin, grow in grace, and increase in holiness.

Is your prayer the same as Paul's prayer? If you are praying for the sanctification of the church, then you must be praying for the edification of the church and not the destruction of the church.

7. Special Relationships

And the Scripture was fulfilled which says, "Abraham believed God, and it was accounted to him for righteousness." And he was called the friend of God.

James 2:23

True friends are scarce. The old cynic who went about in broad daylight with a lighted lantern in search of a friend would have difficulty in finding a true friend. It has often been said, "I went out to find a friend, but could not find one there. I went out to be a friend and friends were everywhere." How does the Bible relate the concept of friendship? The Bible is as up to date as the newspaper.

True friendship often assumes a rough garb. The Bible says "Faithful are the wounds of a friend" (Proverbs 27:6). The wounds may come in the form of rebuke or correction. The Lord Jesus Christ said, "If your brother sins go and reprove him in private; if he listens to you, you have won your brother. But if he does not listen to you, take one or two more with you, so that by the mouth of two or three witnesses every fact may be confirmed" (Matthew 18:15-16). True friends will follow the teaching of Scripture. They will help each other as they struggle with the old sin nature, but if they are true friends they will follow the teaching of Scripture. Go to your friend "in private." Unfortunately, many friendships are severed because one or the other did not follow the teaching of Scripture and go "in private." The result is often gossip and slander.

The church is in the public arena. The people and events associated with church life become the objects of either praise or scorn. The praiseworthy church reflects the character of God's law in worship and morality. The church that becomes the object of scorn reflects the character of Satan's deceptive devices.

The public sector judges the church based on the public lives of its members. Specific sins such as gossip and slander practiced or known to be practiced by persons in the church bring great disgrace to the church. Gossip is most often associated with someone spreading a rumor, which means a story, or statement is circulated without any confirmation or certainty. Slander is a false or defamatory statement.

The Bible always uses the word "gossip" in a bad sense. In 1 Timothy 3:11 women are told not to be malicious gossips. In 2 Timothy 3:3 the word "malicious gossip" is used universally to apply to men and women. The Greek word diabolos translates to the English "gossip" in both texts. The Greek word diabolos is also translated "the devil" 34 times in the New Testament. We get the English word diabolic from the Greek diabolos. Obviously the apostle Paul intended to convey the wickedness of "malicious gossip."

The Bible uses the word slander in a most negative sense. In fact the wisdom writer has said, "He who spreads slander is a fool." The Psalmist said, "The fool has said in his heart, there is no God." In either case the fool has no positive witness for the Lord God Almighty. Slander is particularly detestable because it has the smell of murder. To slander a person and destroy his name is not just a violation of the ninth commandment, but also the sixth commandment.

Gossip and slander are common sins in many churches today. However, because of the nature of these sins, they are very difficult to discipline. If the gossip is within the confines of the church, discipline is relatively simple. Just follow the instructions in Matthew 18. Follow them after consulting the full counsel of God, such as the text in Galatians 6:1-2, especially verse 2. Also check Matthew 6:15. The more you study Scripture the bigger the snowball gets.

However, if the gossip is spread from within the church to those out of the church, it is merely hearsay and the third party outside the church refuses to reveal the spreader of the gossip, so the church suffers because of the sin of one of its members.

Gossip and slander have an advocate and his name is Satan. He deceives people into thinking that it is permissible to gossip, slander, and therefore break the sixth and ninth commandments. John Calvin mentions a more applicable purpose in his commentary to 1 Timothy 5:19: "He now tells Timothy not to let them [elders] be exposed to slanderous attacks or burdened with unsubstantiated and unsupported accusations...For none are more to guard against malice of men in this way. For none are more exposed to slander and insults than godly teachers ...It is indeed a trick of Satan to estrange men from their minister so as gradually to bring their teaching into contempt." The apostle Peter inferred that Christians would be slandered as evildoers (2 Peter 2:12). The Psalmist said no less in Psalm 41:5: "My enemies speak evil against me..."

Godly ministers, elders, deacons, and church members will be the subject of gossip and slander if they preach, teach, and believe the full counsel of God. It may be properly called the battle of the tongues. The godly man seeks the truth from the Word of

God. The slanderous man wants to have his own way apart from the Word of God. Since truth is not on his side, he must lie to get a hearing. The writer of Proverbs explains: "A worthless man digs up evil, while his words are as a scorching fire. A perverse man spreads strife, and a slanderer separates intimate friends" (Proverbs 16:27-28). Gossip and slander are terrible sins, but they are not unforgivable sins unless they are against the Holy Spirit. When the gossiper or slanderer becomes aware of his or her sin, he or she must immediately ask forgiveness from the person about whom he or she spread the gossip or slander.

A friend is like a whetstone that gives keenness to the edge of energy and life. The Bible says, "Iron sharpens iron, so one man sharpens another" (Proverbs 27:17). There are many examples of this aphorism in the Bible. We find David and Jonathan, Ruth and Naomi, or perhaps Paul and Timothy just to mention a few. A friend can encourage when things are difficult, wearisome, or painful. A friend can comfort and advise during the trials of life. Friends make up for each other's defects and they delight in their friendship.

Friends not only learn from each other, they help each other develop character. That process will always be demonstrated by faithfulness. One could not but be moved by the story of a soldier who asked his officer if he might go out into the "no man's land" between the trenches in World War I to bring in one of his comrades who lay grievously wounded. "You can go," said the officer, "but it is not worth it. Your friend is probably dead and you will throw your own life away." However, the man went. Somehow he managed to get to his friend, hoist him on to his shoulder, and bring him back to the trenches. The two of them tumbled in together and lay in the trench bottom. The officer looked very tenderly on the rescuer and then he said, "I told you it wouldn't be worth it. Your friend is dead and you are mortally wounded." The soldier replied, "It was worth it." "How was it worth it?" asked the officer. The soldier replied "it was worth it because when I got to him he was still alive, and he said to me, 'Jim I knew you'd come.'"

The cutting edge of friendship may be found in the form of wounds, encouragement, and faithfulness. Be a friend, it is worth the effort.

The fourth chapter of John is an account of Jesus as he encounters a woman at the well of Samaria. The Samaritans were despised by the Jews, but Jesus being a Jew, seemed not to despise them. In fact when Jesus went to Samaria, he went about to explain the gospel to a Samaritan woman. This woman was living in an adulterous relationship and, no doubt, a disgrace to the community. Little did it matter to Jesus that this woman was a social low-class. Did social peer pressure keep Jesus from going to Samaria? No! Just the opposite. He went to Samaria to be a friend to the Samaritans. The special relationship that friends have ought to be a matter of public display. Unfortunately any display of affection is not considered the norm in American Christianity. Forget the norm and consider the Word of God. There is a commandment often overlooked that commands Christians to "Greet one another with a holy kiss" (Romans 16:16). Even macho Peter the apostle commands Christians to "Greet one another with a kiss of love" (1 Peter 5:14). This practice was eastern cultural tradition practiced long before it was commanded in the New Testament. The kiss was a holy or to use more religious language it was a sacred kiss. It was a symbol of fellowship and union based on reconciliation. To greet one another with a holy kiss expresses mutual affection and equality before God. Some biblical expositors dismiss the command and argue that it was a cultural symbol. They argue that there is a vast cultural chasm between the early church and the 20th cen. church.

This past century has produced an abundance of literature about the subject of friendship. Much of it has been and still is under the heading of relational theology. This is an approach to Christianity that stresses the relationship of persons to persons rather than doctrinal belief and a direct relationship to God. Religious leaders have been very successful in propagating this psychological concept, but it proves to be counter productive.

The problem is that the biblical sense of friendship is lost to a utilitarian arrangement or to say it another way, friendship is merely for convenience. People want to be friends and have friends because of the advantages afforded by the friendship itself. That is not biblical, nor is it a principle of ethics that is normative in any sense. Unfortunately, too many people allege friendship just to take advantage of and use other people. Friendship results from the desire to serve, not to be served.

Where does this friendship business end? There is no end to friendship. It only has a beginning point. Older friends may depart and go to be with God, but the friendship remains. New friends must be made because there is always a desire for friendship to fulfill an emptiness that is often called loneliness.

Enrich your life by looking for friendships the way Jesus looked for them. He went to "out of the way" places like Samaria. He sought to be a friend to people regardless of their demeanor or circumstances in life. An English publication offered a prize for the best definition of a friend, and among the thousands of answers the winner defined a friend. "A friend, - the one who comes in when the whole world has gone out." Go to Samaria and be a friend.

8. The Most Wanted

Therefore, as the elect of God, holy and beloved, put on tender mercies, kindness, humility, meekness, longsuffering; bearing with one another, and forgiving one another, if anyone has a complaint against another; even as Christ forgave you, so you also must do. But above all these things put on love, which is the bond of perfection. And let the peace of God rule in your hearts, to which also you were called in one body; and be thankful. Let the word of Christ dwell in you richly in all wisdom, teaching and admonishing one another in psalms and hymns and spiritual songs, singing with grace in your hearts to the Lord. And whatever you do in word or deed, do all in the name of the Lord Jesus, giving thanks to God the Father through Him.

Colossians 3:12-17

The FBI has a list of the ten most wanted criminals. Everyone probably has a list of things that they want the most. Sometimes it is a wish list and other times it may be a list of household chores. A list is said to make life a little simpler. There was a time when life was simple. For instance life was once simple in small town America. It has been said that you know you are in a small town when:

- You don't use your turn signal because everyone knows where you're going.

- You dial the wrong number and talk 15 minutes anyway.

- You write a check on the wrong bank and the check is covered for you.

- You drive into the ditch five miles out of town and people in town know it before you get home.

- You miss a Sunday at church and receive a get-well card.

- Someone asks you how you feel and then listens to what you say.

Nostalgia, perhaps, but more truth than not. The small town illustration point us to the most wanted gems in all of life. We all crave for sincere and open relationships. Simple relationships are like the sweet water of life. Human relationships for Christian men and women are expressed according to the condition of the heart. The heart refers to the soul, sometimes referred to as the heart, consisting of the mind, will, and emotions. You can have sincere and open relationships if you will let the peace of Christ rule in your hearts.

Relationship skills are absolutely necessary for the well-being of God's people. However, a right relationship with God is necessary to exercise the skills necessary for right relationships with one another in the body of Christ. Most people have a fear of being rejected when threatened with a new relationship. The fear of failure is the offspring of Satan's lie in the Garden of Eden. Before our first parents fell into sin, they had perfect relationships. Nothing was hidden. After they sinned they hid, from God, and each other. The fear of failure in relationships has plagued the human race since that time.

Inadequate relationship skills result in a large number of divorces in this country. They fail to work out relationship rules that may be found in the Word of God. Children reject parental authority and fail to follow relationship rules. Pastors move from one church to another because pastors and congregations fail to follow God's relationship rules. Developing relationship skills will work to your advantage, if you follow the rulebook that God gives His people.

I'm amazed at how seriously we follow the advice of a medical doctor. You need medication, so the doctor prescribes it and you are faithful to follow the directions. But when it comes to God instructing us, we give a causal listen and then go on our way, unless of course, it is convenient to do what God says do.

Christians can have the most wanted of all virtues by following the instructions gives to them. It all starts with, "Let the peace of God rule in your hearts." The peace of God does not refer to peace with Christ; that is what happens when God saves you. The "peace of God" means you are free because you laid aside the old self and the evil practices that accompany the old self. The capstone of the Christian experience is to let God decide how you must live your life. If you let God control your whole being, your relationship skills will increase significantly.

The basis upon which all human relationships are built is sacrificial love. Christian's who love each other particularly demonstrate love by forgiving each other. Relationships will be unique and special if you follow this rule, forgiving each other, but every relationship will fail if Christians do not forgive one another. Mutual forgiveness means that if you have to forgive today, it is likely that you will need to be forgiven tomorrow.

If you "Let the peace of God rule in your hearts" it should naturally follow that you "Let the word of Christ richly dwell within." The word of Christ probably refers to the nature, character, person and work of Jesus Christ. Christians depend on the richness of the word of Christ to enhance the quality of relationships. If Christians do not feast upon the Word of God then they do not know how to relate to one another about spiritual things.

If the Christian has a most wanted list, I'm sure there are two things that are most wanted:

- The peace of God ruling your heart.
- The word of Christ richly dwelling within you.

These most wanted virtues are a great asset to the Christian. The peace of God prevails when love produces forgiveness. The word of Christ prevents us from believing a false gospel. Both the peace of God and the word of Christ profoundly influence our relationship skills.

Clara Barton, founder of the American Red Cross was once reminded by a friend of how someone had hurt her years before. "Don't you remember the wrong done to you?" The friend asked. "No," Clara replied, "I distinctly remember forgetting that." I don't know if Clara Barton was a Christian, but she was practicing God's commandment by letting the peace of God rule in her heart.

Christian relationships built on the Word of God will lead to unity in the church. Although perfect unity among God's people is impossible, there is a perfect unity among the trinity, God the Father, God the Son, and God the Holy Spirit. I have often heard it said, "If you find the perfect church, don't join it because you will destroy the perfection."

Unity is a gift from God that grows if Christians follow the right relationship rules. The Puritan pastor, Richard Baxter, asked a profound question in one of his sermons. "If we saw God, and heaven, and hell before us, do you think it would effectually reconcile our differences and heal our unbrotherly exasperations and divisions?"

The love of Christ is the primary benefit for the Christian who is in union with Christ. Unity with Christ is certain to sooth any dissension among the brethren in Christ. John Calvin said, "It is strange if Christ, whom we preach as our peace, and who, removing the ground of disagreement, appeased to us our Father in Heaven, do not also cause us mutually to cultivate brotherly peace on earth."

Paul wrote the Philippian church and said, "if there is any fellowship of the Spirit if any affection and mercy, fulfill my joy by being like-minded…" (Philippians 2:1-2). The word "if" assumes the condition is affirmative. If there is and there is "be like-minded." The word fellowship describes a partnership, a binding relationship among two or more people. Christians should have fellowship of the spirit because it is the same Holy Spirit that converts us. It is the same Holy Spirit that empowers us. You don't have one type of the Holy Spirit in you and another type of the Holy Spirit in me. We all share in the same Holy Spirit. The fellowship of the Spirit should lead us into the unity of the faith and the knowledge of the Son of God.

J. C. Ryle was correct when he said, "The utter absence of real charity and love among men in the days when our Lord was upon earth ought not be overlooked. Well would it be if men had never quarreled about religion after He left the world! Quarrels among the crew of a sinking ship are not more hideous, unseemly and irrational than the majority of quarrels among professors of religion."

Get rid of the unwanted list:

Strife
Selfish ambition
Conceit
Dissension
Self-interest

Get out the most wanted list:

The peace of God ruling your heart
The word of Christ richly dwelling within you.

9. A Heavy Load

Come to Me, all you who labor and are heavy laden, and I will give you rest. Take My yoke upon you and learn from Me, for I am gentle and lowly in heart, and you will find rest for your souls. For My yoke is easy and My burden is light.
Matthew 11:28-30

A farm worker carrying a bag of potatoes on his back was asked by a skeptic: "How do you know you are saved?" The worker took a few steps and then dropped the bag. Then he said, "How do I know I've dropped the bag without looking around to see." The skeptic replied, "You can tell by reducing the weight." The worker was quick to respond, "And that is how I know I'm saved. I have lost the guilty feeling of sin and sorrow and have found peace and satisfaction in my Lord and Savior." The saving grace of God removes the heavy load of guilt. Have you ever experienced the removal of a heavy burden? The relief from a heavy burden will change your outlook on life.

The ripening age of modernity has brought all the ills that come with modernization and technology. The age of consumerism is a huge load to bear. It is a real burden to keep up with the next door neighbor. The postmodern culture burdens Christians with a make-believe world. Do you know how hard it is to believe something that is unbelievable? The burden of the success syndrome weighs heavily on the yoke of most Americans. Then there is the burden of feeling victimized by the special interest groups. The burden of psychological disorders is greater than previously known to man. The burden of civil and social disorder increase exponentially each day.

The concept of being burdened is certainly not new and I think Jesus realized that when He uttered these profound words, "My yoke is easy and My burden is light." The purpose of a yoke was to distribute the weight equally upon a person's shoulders. However, even with a good yoke an excessive weight causes pain and distress.

Jesus was speaking to the oppressed, the one suffering pain and distress, when He said His burden was light. The burdens of life are many, but most of them are insignificant compared to a Christian burdened by sin.

Paul the apostle wrote the Church at Galatia and said, "Brethren, if a man is overtaken in any trespass, you who are spiritual restore such a one in a spirit of gentleness, considering yourself lest you also be tempted. Bear one another's burdens, and so fulfill the law of Christ" (Galatians 6:1 – 2).

In the immediate context, a Christian is burdened with sin. Preachers and Bible Teachers abuse this command, bear one another's burdens, on a regular basis. They often interpret this text to refer to some physical or material need. The context refers to a spiritual need, especially spiritual help for one who is burdened with sin. It is nonsense to say, "I'm not burdened with sin." The Bible states the absolute truth. "For all have sinned and fall short of the glory of God" (Romans 3:23). I need to mention some important aspects of grammar in that text. The words "have sinned" and "fall short" are action words, commonly known as verbs. "Have sinned" refers to the past time for "all" human beings, except Jesus Christ. "Fall short" refers to the present time for "all" human beings, except Jesus Christ. If you believe you are not a sinner then you must be Jesus Christ. In his book "Three Free Sins" Steve Brown, speaking of himself as a pastor/preacher said, "Trying to teach people not to sin and, at the same time, finding out that they are still sinning is not a fulfilling task. Neither is trying to cover up that you have your own sins too (maybe bigger than your students'/parishioners')." The fact that sin is, should not be a question. The question ought to be, "how may I help my Christian brother or sister who is burdened with sin?"

It is easy to ignore one who has fallen into sin. "He deserves it, let him work it out," is the easy way out. It is much easier to expect other Christians to help the poor old sinner, rather than you getting involved. It is much easier to criticize them or find fault. When a Christian brother is overtaken by sin, what should Christians do? There are two extremes to this question. One extreme is to punish the sinner rather than restore the sinner. However, remember the old saying, "what goes around comes around." The other extreme is to ignore the sinning brother or sister. The biblical and compassionate solution is to bear one another's sin burden. It does not mean to agree with sin, but offer mutual help to restore one burdened with sin.

Interpersonal relationships are strained because of sin. Unfortunately "bearing one another's sin burden, may lead to utilitarianism. To put it another way one person may offer to help another with the hope of gaining a favor.

Why is a Christian burdened with sin? Sin all started with Adam and Eve. The theologians call it original sin; Adam's sin was imputed to all men. To put it another way we inherited the guilt of

Adam's sin, and the corruption of sin. However, Adam is not to take all the blame because we actually sin by violating God's law.

There are many different kinds of sins. There are sins of omission and commission. One means we do not do what we should do and the other is we do what God told us not to do. For instance, Christ gave us a positive command to make disciples. If we fail to make disciples, it is a sin of omission. The Bible says, "Do not bear false witness". When we fail to keep this commandment, it is a sin of commission. In the midst of sin and confusion, how can we deal with the problem of sin? Is there any hope for us Christians? Yes, there is hope and it is found in the Word of God.

Godly Christians should help restore or as the New International Version interprets the text, "gently and humbly help him back unto the right path." Extend help to the brother so that he may overcome his spiritual weakness. We are commanded in Scripture to bear one another's sin burden. The reason we are commanded to bear one another burdens is not for practical benevolent purposes. We bear one another's burdens to fulfill the Law of Christ. The law of Christ is a reflection of God's love in our lives.

John 13:34 - Love one another

James 2:8 - Love your neighbor as yourself

Galatians 5:14 - Love your neighbor as yourself

There is a sense in which the law of Christ weighs heavy upon our soul. The law of Christ is not a burden, but a sense of responsibility to keep this law. It sure sounds pious to say, "I love my neighbor as much as I love myself", but it is merely a sound.

The weight of the Law of Christ is heavy, especially heavy on the soul of a sinner and we are all sinners.

Evaluate your own life by the law of Christ before you try to bear the burden of another sinner. Ask yourself the question. Are you spiritual? Do you reflect love and joy in your life? Do you have peace with other Christians? Do you treat other Christians with kindness, goodness, faithfulness, gentleness, and self-control?

We fulfill the law of Christ, our love for one another, by our kindness. Christians often forget an eternal principle as explained by Dr. Luke in this manner, For everyone to whom much is given, from him much will be required." As God is kind to you, then you must be kind to others. If God has given you much, do you give much more?

We fulfill the law of Christ by our faithfulness. "Truly God is good to Israel, to such as are pure in heart" (Psalm 73:1). "But You, O God the Lord, Deal with me for Your name's sake; because Your mercy is good" (Psalm 109:21). In proportion to the mercy God has shown to you, do you show mercy to others?

We fulfill the law of Christ by our faithfulness. Our faithfulness to God will evidence itself according to our relationship with Him. Faithfulness to God is a full time activity.

Gentleness and self-control are aspects of the law of Christ that are closely related. We must be gentle with one another while remembering the virtue to keep our mind and conduct in check.

The self-test comes from Paul's letter to the Galatians. "But the fruit of the Spirit is love, joy, peace, longsuffering, kindness, goodness, faithfulness, gentleness, self-control. Against such there is no law" (Galatians 5:22-23). Evaluate yourselves by these standards. If you pass the test then you can help your stumbling brother. However, if you are stumbling as much as your brother, calamity will be the result. If you are not doing these things you cannot help your brother or bear his burdens. Find someone to help you bear your sin burden before you try to pick up the heavy burden of your brother.

Before we can fulfill the law of Christ, we must consider the other persons life style from a true biblical perspective. This is most difficult if we are to bear one another's burdens. Evaluation of self is easy, because we know us. "But let each one examine his own work, and then he will have rejoicing in himself alone, and not in another" (Galatians 6:4). It is perfectly legitimate to rejoice in God's grace and mercy; rejoice in your own Christian life. The law of Christ will never rejoice in the fall and sins of others.

We are especially warned about the manner in which we bear one another's burdens. Spiritual pride may be a temptation that is spiritually dangerous. The way to help a brother or sister with the sin burden is with gentleness and compassion.

A skilled surgeon may give these words of assurance before he performs a delicate operation: I may hurt you, but I will not injure you." Bearing one another's burden may be painful, but it is not harmful.

Christ redeemed God's children by bearing the burden of sin for them. His grace, mercy, love, and compassion hanging on the cross was the ultimate bearing their burden of sin.

10. Spiritual Patriotism

And I told them of the hand of my God which had been good upon me, and also of the king's words that he had spoken to me. So they said, "Let us rise up and build." Then they set their hands to this good work.

Nehemiah 2:18

Have you ever wondered what happened to the fifty-six men who signed the declaration of Independence? Five were captured by the British and tortured to death. Twelve had their home ransacked and burned. Nine fought and died from wounds or the hardships of the revolutionary war. Carter Braxton of Virginia, a wealthy planter and trader, saw his ships swept from the seas by the British navy. He sold his home and properties to pay his debts and died in rags. Thomas McKeam was so hounded by the British that he was forced to move his family almost constantly. He served in Congress without pay, and his family was kept in hiding. His possessions were taken from him and poverty was his reward. When Thomas Nelson Jr. discovered that the British had taken over the Nelson home as their headquarters, Nelson quietly urged General George Washington to open fire, which was done. The home was destroyed and Nelson died bankrupt. (Taken from the Essay, *The Price They Paid*). These men were known as American patriots.

Webster defines a patriot as "a person who loves, supports, and defends his country and its interests with devotion." The patriots of the American Revolution signed the Declaration of Independence "for the support of this declaration, with a firm reliance on the protection of the Divine Providence, we mutually pledge to each other, our lives, our fortunes and our sacred honor." These patriots pledged and sacrificed for the mere existence of nation, a nation that cease to exist. The church is eternal. It will never end. So, where are the spiritual patriots?

Adlai Stevenson once said, "I venture to say that patriotism is not a short frenzied outburst of emotion but the tranquil and steady dedication of a lifetime." He is right and it is especially true for spiritual patriots. For spiritual patriots it will be a lifetime of devotion. The Bible has a repertoire of spiritual patriots. Nehemiah is a good example of a spiritual patriot. Nehemiah's spiritual patriotism was to God and to God's people. He proved his patriotism by his lifelong dedication to serving God for the benefit of God's people.

A spiritual patriot will always have an interest in God's kingdom. Nehemiah was among the Israelites who found themselves in captivity because of their rebellion against God. However, Nehemiah was the cupbearer for the king of Babylon. Nehemiah was in a most honored position in the court of the most powerful monarch in the world. However, Nehemiah did not forget that he was a child of God and at that God's people were disenfranchised from the land of promise and a place to worship the true God. Nehemiah was careful to inquire about the condition of his homeland and prayed for God's grace. The report was not good. "And they said to me, 'The survivors who are left from the captivity in the province are there in great distress and reproach. The wall of Jerusalem is also broken down, and its gates are burned with fire'" (Nehemiah 1:3). Christians ought to have an interest in the condition of the church, locally and globally. The spiritual health of the church depends on spiritual patriots who will be grieved when they discover the poor spiritual condition of the church. " So it was, when I heard these words, that I sat down and wept, and mourned for many days; I was fasting and praying before the God of heaven" (Nehemiah 1:4).

A spiritual patriot will confess as Nehemiah confessed. "I pray before You now, day and night, for the children of Israel Your servants, and confess the sins of the children of Israel which we have sinned against You. Both my father's house and I have sinned. We have acted very corruptly against You, and have not kept the commandments, the statutes, nor the ordinances which You commanded Your servant Moses" (Nehemiah 1:1-7). The spirituality of the church may be compromised, if spiritual patriots do not confess their sins and recognize the sins of their previous generation.

Spiritual patriots must be willing to work to restore the church to good spiritual health. Nehemiah returned to Jerusalem, spent a few days praying, meditating, and assessing the condition of the city. Then he told the people "You see the distress that we are in, how Jerusalem lies waste, and its gates are burned with fire. Come and let us build the wall of Jerusalem, that we may no longer be a reproach" (Nehemiah 2:17). The response from the people is what you would expect from spiritual patriots. "So they said, 'Let us rise up and build.' Then they set their hands to this good work" (Nehemiah 2:18).

Spiritual patriots are kingdom builders. Tools are necessary for the builders to be effective. First, they must be enabled to do the work. The Holy Spirit takes care of the enabling and the builder does the work. Then the builder needs a plan approved by the owner of the kingdom; it is called the Bible. It sounds simple; just follow the plan and do the work. Spiritual patriots must be very careful to avoid cosmetic coverings. The owner can tell the difference between the fake and the true.

Resistance is inevitable when spiritual patriots begin kingdom work. Adversaries challenged Nehemiah on several occasions. Sometimes the enemy will be forthright and other times may appear as wolves in sheep's clothing. When World War 1 broke out, the War ministry in London sent a coded message to the British outpost in an inaccessible area of Africa. The message read: War declared. Arrest all enemy aliens in your district. The War ministry received a prompt reply from one district. Have arrested 10 Germans, 6 Belgians, 4 Frenchmen, 2 Italians, 3 Austrians, and 1 American. Please advise immediately who we are at war with. Sometimes it is difficult to identify the enemy, because they disguise themselves.

There is an old saying that "Little men cause big problems." For instance, a man was born in Austria April 20, 1889. His family was poor. As a student, he was a failure and never completed high school. He lived in Vienna until 1913 living on an orphan's pension. He served in World War 1, but was never promoted above private 1st class, because his superiors thought he lacked leadership ability. He became involved in political activity and was soon sentenced to five years imprisonment for attempting to overthrow the government. After he was appointed Chancellor of Germany, he quickly established himself as dictator. You know the rest of the story about Adolf Hitler. Little men do cause big problems.

Throughout history, little men have caused big problem in every level of society and in every cultural milieu. Little men like Charles Darwin infecting the minds of young professing Christians.

William James and his philosophy of pragmatism has likewise infiltrated the institutes of higher learning, which eventually infected Christian educational institutions. If spiritual patriots work in any kingdom project, they will face opposition from the enemy. It may come from within the church or from those outside the church.

God calls every child of God to be a spiritual patriot and kingdom worker. Seek the counsel of the pastor and elders of the church to confirm your particular gift(s) and the exercise of your gift(s) in the kingdom of God. Before you begin your work take time to rest, pray, and plan. "The plans of the diligent lead surely to plenty, but those of everyone who is hasty, surely to poverty" (Proverbs21:5). Investigate the training and preparation necessary to make your kingdom gift useful. Inform others of your plan. Set a reasonable goal for your part in the kingdom work.

There are too many stories of professing Christians having begun a work that ended in physical pain and emotional suffering. Sometimes Christians fail to recognize their gifts and abilities. Then they tend to look for help in the wrong places. Bozo the Clown went to a psychologist seeking help to overcome his depression. The doctor told him to go see Bozo the Clown. His reply was "I am Bozo the clown." A spiritual patriot must seek counsel from other qualified spiritual patriots and plan according to King's blueprint.

Spiritual patriots should guard against the swelled-head syndrome otherwise known as arrogance and self-importance. The story is told of a physics professor and his chauffeur. The professor was on a lecture circuit visiting major universities. The professor used the same lecture notes at each university. His chauffeur had a sharp mind and over a period of time he memorized the professor's lecture. While traveling to the prestigious Massachusetts Institute of Technology the chauffeur challenged the professor. "Why I could give that lecture if people didn't know I was your chauffeur. The professor remembered the planned format at MIT so he thought to himself, "I'll fix him." They agreed to change positions. The chauffeur delivered a flawless lecture. At the end of his lecture, the master of ceremonies did something the chauffeur did not expect. He opened the floor to questions. One man stood up and asked a question about quantum physics that the chauffeur could not answer. The swelled-head syndrome is particularly contagious among church leaders. Spiritual patriotism will always be accompanied with humility.

Spiritual Patriots will have a passion for divine truth. The Bible is the only source for God's divine truth. Along with the Holy Spirit attesting its truth, it has words that convict, convince and comfort. However, more importantly divine truth is necessary to reform and restore individual Christians and churches so they can be witnesses of God's grace and peace.

Spiritual patriots ought to distinguish words that are useful and correct the misuse of words. The word liberal and its extended world and life view known as liberalism have changed through the years. There was a time when the word liberal was a very good and useful word. The English word liberal comes from the Latin word "libero" which means to set free. From libero, we get English words like liberty and liberal. If you look in a book of synonyms under the word liberal, you will find words like unselfish, kind, tolerant, and generous. Hmm...Those words sound like words that describe a spiritual patriot. Political, social, and religious liberalism are pejorative terms in this present day, but if the modern day use was applied to the 16th century, the Roman Catholic Church may have called Martin Luther and John Calvin religious liberals. The English Throne may have called George Washington a political liberal. Alexis de Tocqueville may have been called a social liberal. If we go back to the classical meaning of the word liberal, we would discover that it referred to one who was not restrained by the contemporary establishment. Christians have the unique and inerrant volume of words that are true in every age. It is called the Bible. A spiritual Patriot will be a true liberal. He or she will be unselfish, kind, tolerant, and generous, but he or she will conserve the truth of God's Word. The church needs spiritual patriots that are liberal conservatives.

God has chosen Spiritual patriots to work in His vineyard. "So they said, 'Let us rise up and build.' Then they set their hands to this good work."

11. Secure Investments

I appeal to you for my son Onesimus, whom I have begotten while in my chains, who once was unprofitable to you, but now is profitable to you and to me. I am sending him back. You therefore receive him, that is, my own heart, whom I wished to keep with me, that on your behalf he might minister to me in my chains for the gospel. But without your consent I wanted to do nothing, that your good deed might not be by compulsion, as it were, but voluntary. For perhaps he departed for a while for this purpose, that you might receive him forever, no longer as a slave but more than a slave—a beloved brother, especially to me but how much more to you, both in the flesh and in the Lord.

Philemon 10-16

"I invest in annuities" was Phil's response to the question his friend asked, "where do you invest your money." Phil believed that annuities were secure investments. In the world of finance, Phil may be right, but life consists of more than financial investments. Although he never mentioned financial investments, the apostle Paul was eternally investing. Paul was an investor because he invested in the lives of people for the sake of the Kingdom of God. Paul's investments were secure investments.

I will use the following illustration to show the results of investing in your children.

In 1900, A.E. Winship published a comparative study of two patriarchs and their posterity—Jonathan Edwards and Max

Jukes, a lazy Dutch criminal and ne'er do well—to show the importance of heredity and education. The challenge for culturalists such as Winship, faced with "vast multitudes" coming from abroad bringing moral and physical disease, was "of making regenerates out of degenerates." The claims of the social benefits of "pure blood" were the targets of criticism and satire even back then (the controversial and outspoken lawyer Clarence Darrow--who was defense attorney at the famous Scopes "Monkey" trial in Tennessee in 1925--would later write that he'd rather have had Max Jukes than Jonathan Edwards as a neighbor). In fact, the "Jukes" was an amalgam of a number of families, and eugenicists and genealogists alike ignored or glossed over the fact that Edwards's grandmother was probably emotionally disturbed and members of her family were guilty of axe-murder and infanticide, that Edwards's own son, Pierpont, was a libertine; and his grandson, Aaron Burr, a freethinker who killed Alexander Hamilton in an infamous duel. Social engineering, then, became one of the more unusual—and unexpected—ways that Edwards was appropriated as a cultural symbol.

Below are excerpts from Winship's work, *Jukes-Edwards: A Study in Education and Heredity*, illustrating the bias from which he approached his subjects:

. . . In view of what has been learned regarding Jonathan Edwards, his ancestors and his children, his grandchildren might have found some excuse for presuming upon the capacity and character which they inherited. In their veins was the blood of famous lines of noble men and women; the blood of Edwards, Stoddard, Pierpont, and Hooker was thrilling in their thought and intensifying their character. They had inherited capacity and character at their best, but they did not presume upon it. If ever inheritance would justify indifference to training, it was in the case of the grandchildren of Jonathan Edwards, but they were far from indifferent to their responsibility. . . .

The "Jukes" had no inherited capacity or training upon which they could safely presume. Their only chance lay in nursing every germ of hope by means of industry or education, through the discipline of the shop, the training of the schools, and the inspiration of the church. Did they appreciate it? Far from it. Instead of developing capacity by training, not one of the 1,200 secured even a moderate education, and only twenty of them ever had a trade, and ten of these learned it in the state prison.

On the other hand, although the Edwards family inherited abundant capacity and character, every child has been educated from early childhood. Not all of the college members of the family have been discovered, and yet among the men alone I have found 285 graduates and a surprisingly large number of these have supplemented the college course with post-graduate or professional study. Just as the "Jukes" have intensified their degeneracy by neglect, the Edwards family has magnified capacity and character by industry and education.

Among the 285 college graduates of the Edwards family there are thirteen presidents of college and other higher institutions of learning, sixty-five professors of colleges, and many principals of important academies and seminaries. Forty-five American and foreign colleges and universities have this family among the alumni.

It has already been emphasized that the Jukes always mingled blood of their own quality in their descendants, and that the Edwards family has invariably chosen blood of the same general tone and force. Who can think for a moment that the Jukes would have remained on so low a level if the Edwards blood had been mixed with theirs, or that the Edwards would have retained their intellectual supremacy if they had married into the Jukes. The fact is that in 150 years the Jukes never did mingle first-class blood with their own, and the Edwards family has not in 150 years degenerated through marriage.

It is pre-eminently true that a mighty intellectual and moral force does plough the channel of its thought and character through many generations. It would be well for any doubter to study the records of thoroughbreds in the animal world. The highest record ever made for milk and butter was by an animal of no family, and she was valuable only for what she could earn. None of her power went to her offspring. She was simply a high-toned freak, but an animal with a clean pedigree back to some great progenitor is valuable independently of individual earning qualities.

No more would any one claim that the Jukes would not have been immensely improved by education and environment, or that the Edwards family could have maintained its record without education, training, and environment. The facts show that the Jukes first, last, and all the time neglected these advantages, and that the Edwards family, with all its intermarrying, has never neglected them.

The Jukes were notorious law breakers, while the Edwards family has furnished practically no lawbreakers, and a great array of more than 100 lawyers, thirty judges, and the most eminent law professor probably in the country. . . .

When one studies the legal side of the [Edwards] family it seems as though they were instinctively and chiefly lawyers and judges. It simply means that whatever the Edwards family has done it has done ably and nobly. . . .

Of the Jukes, 440 were more or less viciously diseased. The Edwards family was healthy and long lived. Of the eleven children of Mr. and Mrs. Edwards, four lived to be more seventy years of age . . . The record for health and longevity continues through every generation. They have also done much to alleviate the sufferings of mankind. There have been sixty physicians, all marked men . . .

The Jukes neglected all religious privileges, defied and antagonized the church and all that it stands for, while the Edwards family has more than a hundred clergymen, missionaries, and theological professors, many of the most eminent in the country's history. . . .

Not one of the Jukes was ever elected to a public office, while more than eighty of the family of Jonathan Edwards have been especially honored. Legislatures in all sections of the country, governor's councils, state treasuries, and other elective offices have been filled by these men. . . . They have represented the United States at several foreign court; several have been members of congress; three have been United States senators; and one vice-president of the United States.

The Jukes lacked the physical and moral courage, as well as the patriotic purpose, to enlist, but there were seventy-five officers in the army and navy from the family of Mr. Edwards. This family has been prominent as officers, chaplains, or surgeons, in the army and navy in the three great wars. . .

The Jukes were as far removed as possible from literature. They not only never created any, but they never read anything that could by any stretch of the imagination be styled good reading. In the Edwards family some sixty have attained prominence in authorship or editorial life. Richard Carvel, is by Mr. Winston Churchill,* a descendant of Mr. Edwards, and I have found 35 books of merit written by the family. Eighteen considerable journals and periodicals have been edited and several important ones founded by the Edwards family.

The Jukes did not wander far from the haunts of Max. They stagnated like the motionless pool, while the Edwards family is a prominent factor in the mercantile, industrial, and professional life of thirty-three states of the union and in several foreign countries, in ninety-two American and many foreign cities. They have been pre-eminently directors of men.

Whatever the Jukes stand for, the Edwards family does not. Whatever weakness the Jukes represent finds its antidote in the Edwards family, which has cost the country nothing in pauperism, in crime, in hospital or asylum service. On the contrary, it represents the highest usefulness in invention, manufacture, commerce, founding of asylums and hospitals, establishing and developing missions, projecting and energizing the best philanthropies. . .(Jonathan Edwards Center, Jonathan Edwards: Family Life, http://edwards.yale.edu/research/about-edwards/family-life).

Investing in the lives of your children is a special privilege. It is special enough to invest time, money, and yes even the whole personality. Jonathan Edwards invested in his children and it paid off for generations. There are occasions when it appears that your investment did not pay dividends. It is then that you have to trust God and remember His word. Proverbs 22:6 - "Train up a child in the way he should go, and when he is old he will not depart from it.

Perfect example in the parable of the rebellious son Luke 15:11-32. The youngest son said to his father, "I want my share of estate now." He took his money took and went to a distant land and wasted all his money. He squandered his money on one party after another. After he lost all his money, a famine hit the land. He ended up working on a hog farm, feeding pigs and was so hungry that he ate pig feed. Then the Bible says "But when he came to his senses, he said, How many of my father's hired men have more than enough bread...I will get up and go to my father..." (Luke 15:11ff).

The young man didn't forget the years that his father had trained him and invested in his life. He knew what kind of man his father was and that he could trust his father. The young man was trained as a child to trust his father. If a child receives the right training early in life, he or she cannot forget it later in life. Maybe reject it, but not forget it.

Although it seems natural to invest in your physical descendents, it is just as important to invest in spiritual children. Paul saw himself as a spiritual father to men like Timothy and Onesimus. He speaks to them tenderly with the kind of love a father has for his own son. Fathers have the opportunity to make the best assets available for an investment in his child or if the father uses counterfeit, the investment is likely to go bankrupt. Paul's letter to Philemon has lessons on being a spiritual father to spiritual children.

Paul was imprisoned at Rome or Ephesus. Onesimus was a slave of Philemon, had probably stolen from Philemon, and ran away from his master. In the providence of God Onesimus and Paul cross paths. Onesimus was converted under the ministry of Paul. The story of Philemon, Paul and Onesimus is a story of a spiritual ministry by a spiritual minister to a spiritual son.

Paul wrote a letter to Philemon; "I appeal to you for my son Onesimus, whom I have begotten while in my chains. Paul does not assume any ability to save anyone. It is God who gives new life to the soul, yet it is by means of man who delivers the Word of God. Paul did not refer to Onesimus as a runaway slave and thief, but called Onesimus "his own son." The Greek word for my son is "teknou" which is a term of endearment. Paul was willing to invest in a runaway slave and thief and then call him my dear son. There is no more precious investment that bringing someone to Jesus Christ. Paul claimed to be the spiritual father to the Corinthian Church. "I do not write these things to shame you, but as my beloved children I warn you. For though you might have ten thousand instructors in Christ, yet you do not have many fathers; for in Christ Jesus I have begotten you through the gospel. Therefore I urge you, imitate me. For this reason I have sent Timothy to you, who is my beloved and faithful son in the Lord, who will remind you of my ways in Christ, as I teach everywhere in every church" (1 Corinthians 4:14-17).

A spiritual child is not only a precious investment; a spiritual child is a profitable investment. Paul wrote Philemon and said Onesimus "is profitable to you and to me." A child of God will be profitable in every way. He or she will take the proper place in God's economy and serve as a servant serves his or her master.

A spiritual child is an eternal investment. Paul sent Onesimus back to Philemon and wrote these words. "For perhaps he (Onesimus) departed for a while for this purpose, that you might receive him forever…"

The divine redemptive grace of Jesus Christ worked to bring about reconciliation because of God's eternal plan. Paul could have said to Onesimus as he said to the Church at Ephesus, "He (God) chose us in Him (Jesus Christ) before the foundation of the world…" (Ephesians 1:4). It was the atoning work of Jesus Christ that brought the slave and master together. Paul must have considered his investment in Onesimus a modest investment, because Christ invested so much more in the apostle Paul.

12. True Religion

He has shown you, O man, what is good; And what does the LORD require of you But to do justly, To love mercy, And to walk humbly with your God?
                                                                Micah 6:8

Religion may be the salt that burns a cut or it may be the sugar that sweetens a bitter lemon. Which religion is your preference, the sweet or the bitter?

Robert Burton's "The Anatomy of Melancholy" analyzes the causes and cures of melancholy, covering a vast scope of scholarship in numerous fields, such as classical studies, theology, philosophy, science, and politics. In his notable work, Burton said, "One religion is as true as another." Almost three centuries later, another English poet wrote: "Religion beats me. I'm amazed at folk drinking the gospels in and never scratching their heads for questions."

Religion is a curiosity among human beings. It is because religion is about what people believe and practice. Every rational creature has a religion of some kind or the other. I've often heard Christians say "I can't discuss Religion with my neighbor." Why? Men and women are passionate about what they believe. Are you passionate about what you believe? God is passionate about what He believes. If man is passionate about what he believes and God is passionate about what He believes, what happens when the two belief systems clash? If there are two belief systems, then there are two religions.

There cannot be two religions in the kingdom of God. False religion has its roots in the lies of Satan. True religion is founded upon God Himself. God was gracious enough to give His people a right understanding of the true religion.

The first point of true religion is that men come to God by faith. Like Abraham, Christians must believe in the Lord and He, (the Lord), will account it to them for righteousness.

The second point of true religion is that men love the grace of God. Therefore, they worship Him like they love Him. Faith, love and worship are inseparable.

Jesus summarized the practice of religion in these terms. "Jesus said to him, 'You shall love the LORD your God with all your heart, with all your soul, and with all your mind.' This is the first and great commandment. And the second is like it: 'You shall love your neighbor as yourself'" (Matthew 22:37-39). True religion excludes self-interest.

If Christians practice religion for self-interest, then it naturally follows that God has a complaint against them. Before the fall of Israel and Judah, God warned His people. "Hear, O you mountains, the LORD's complaint, And you strong foundations of the earth; For the LORD has a complaint against His people, And He will contend with Israel" (Micah 6:2)

God did not list the transgression and sins. He didn't list the violations and offenses. God didn't reprimand them for the countless things they had done to Him, but rather God asks them "What have I done to you?" How have I wearied you? How have I burdened you? (See Micah 6:3).

Those questions suggest that the people were tired of God and His ways. They were bored of God and the routine of worship.

They found it a chore even to the point of weariness to worship him. They wanted something more stimulating, something more interesting, and yes, something that would bring happiness rather than something that would bring goodness. False religion becomes weary with God. False religion becomes bored with God in the routine of worship according to His will. The sin nature inclines rational creatures to practice false religion. The only solution is to turn to God in faith and repentance. Then you will be inclined to practice the true religion. The sin nature will not disappear, but the sinner will have a heart for true religion.

True religion ought to remind Christians of heaven. Do you as an individual Christian actually feel like a heavenly being? Is your family like heaven with no controversy, no conflict, no arguments, and no disagreements? Is your job like heaven? Is your social life like heaven? Is church life like heaven? The answer is no and we grow weary, because of our sinful nature. It seems that heaven is so far away. Is there any hope?

The Bible shows how God redeemed His people from bondage. For instance, God was gracious to the Israelites. He redeemed them from the house of bondage in Egypt. How could they forget that God had saved them from the bonds of slavery? How could they find such a gracious God wearisome and boring? It was easier for God to get his people out of Egypt, than it was to get Egypt out of His people. For that reason, God said, "I have a complaint against My people." So how did God's people respond to God's complaint? There was no shame, no confession of sins, or repentance. All we see from them is arrogance. When God challenged them with their false religion they retorted, God what do you expect of us? Shall I bow before the High God? Shall I bring burnt offerings? Shall I bring some of my best cows? Will you be happy with a 1000 head of sheep? What about 10,000 rivers of soybean oil? Do you want me to sacrifice my first-born son? Literally, the Old Testament Church at Jerusalem said: "God everybody has a price, what is yours?" They thought in terms of a cold hard contract, probably very similar to the thriving business world of that day, rather than a warm genuine tender relationship with the one who created them and gave them their wealth.

I take it they were mocking God by suggesting to offer human sacrifice which was common among the nations around them, but detestable in the eyes of God. Those professing believers thought that ritual, pomp, external and ceremonial religion was the true religion? To put it another way, true religion was simply going through the motions, during the time that Micah ministered to the Old Testament Church.

Then what does God expect of us? "He has shown you, O man, what is good; And what does the LORD require of you But to do justly, To love mercy, And to walk humbly with your God?" (Micah 6:8). God expects His people to do justice. It means to think, speak, and act fairly and honestly towards God and men. Heavy-handed treatment and dishonesty will eventually find its way to the surface and if taken too far it will cause a disaster. Love mercy means to show kindness by forgiving and reconciliation when relationships fall apart. Mercy is the great piece of evidence for true religion. Walk humbly with God means to have a constant sense of your sin before you. It means to have a sense of God's holiness before you. To walk humbly with God means to recognize your weakness and God's power. To walk humbly with God means to acknowledge the saving grace of God in your prosperity and in your adversity. Justice, mercy, and humility is true religion.

Some professing Christians are entangled with the idea that moral principles are the same is true religion. We can be certain that moral principles in Scripture area manifestly perspicuous, but moral principles are not the means of forgiveness and grace. Mercy is the word that many professing Christians have forgotten. However, God said, "For I desire mercy and not sacrifice" (Hosea 6:6). The word mercy comes from a Hebrew word that is translated lovingkindness 176 times in the Old Testament. The instruction from the Word of God is that the "Lord is longsuffering and abundant in mercy [lovingkindness]" (Numbers 14:18) and that the "earth is full of mercy [lovingkindness] of the Lord" (Psalm 33:5).

The mercy of God is at the forefront of your existence. All I have to do is remember God's mercy towards me in the past few minutes and it is overwhelming. Mercy reflects ones love for God and the people that show mercy. To the degree that you love God and your neighbor, then to the same degree you will be able to worship the God of mercy.

Jesus quoted Hosea on two occasions. The first occasion was the call of Matthew the tax collector. The Pharisees (the religious leaders of that day) condemned Jesus for drinking wine and eating with the tax collectors and sinners. Jesus told the morally arrogant religious leaders to go and learn what this means: "I desire mercy and not sacrifice" (Matthew 9:13). On another occasion, the religious leaders confronted Jesus because he violated their unbiblical man-made rules about the Sabbath. Jesus said to the religious leaders: "I say to you that in this place there is One greater than the temple. "But if you had known what this means, 'I desire mercy and not sacrifice' you would not have condemned the guiltless" (Matthew 12:7).

So much for Jesus giving the religious leaders a pat on the back. It was more like a kick in the….well you get the point. The Lord Jesus called the Pharisees children of Satan (John 8:44), yet they were meticulous, so they thought, in the moral standards of the law and ritualistic worship. However, their alleged law keeping and empty ritualism was loathsome to the Lord. It was empty worship because their hearts were empty of lovingkindness. Their compassion for their neighbor was empty.

The remedy for breaking God's law is grace, forgiveness and reconciliation. The remedy for broken relationships is grace, forgiveness, and reconciliation. I must say, the simple things in life are the most difficult to comprehend. The Lord Jesus Christ paid the price for your transgression and sins. Do you believe, then live like you believe.

Faith, love and worship is the foundation for true religion. Jesus said, "You shall love your neighbor as yourself." James applied that commandment and came up with the practice of true religion. "Pure and undefiled religion before God and the Father is this: to visit orphans and widows in their trouble, and to keep oneself unspotted from the world" (James 1:27). Dr. Manford G. Gutzke explained pure and undefiled religion. "Religion is pure if there is nothing selfish in it. It is undefiled if there is nothing proud about it. Our religion is undefiled when our conduct in response to God is not motivated for any personal advantage. The real genuine response to the true God is this; 'to visit the fatherless and the widows in their afflictions.' This includes all people who really need help in their affliction. Visiting them is to come to help them. True religion always buries self. False religion will dig self up from the grave."

Salvation, grace, mercy and peace is the true religion. "In this is love, not that we loved God, but that He loved us and sent His Son to be the propitiation for our sins. Beloved, if God so loved us, we also ought to love one another. No one has seen God at any time. If we love one another, God abides in us, and His love has been perfected in us. By this, we know that we abide in Him, and He in us, because He has given us of His Spirit. And we have seen and testify that the Father has sent the Son as Savior of the world. Whoever confesses that Jesus is the Son of God, God abides in him, and he in God" (1 John 4:15).

13. Marks of a Christian

And seeing the multitudes, He went up on a mountain, and when He was seated His disciples came to Him. Then He opened His mouth and taught them, saying:
  "Blessed are the poor in spirit,
    For theirs is the kingdom of heaven.
  Blessed are those who mourn,
    For they shall be comforted.
  Blessed are the meek,
    For they shall inherit the earth.
  Blessed are those who hunger and thirst for righteousness,
    For they shall be filled.
  Blessed are the merciful,
    For they shall obtain mercy.
  Blessed are the pure in heart,
    For they shall see God.
  Blessed are the peacemakers,
    For they shall be called sons of God.
  Blessed are those who are persecuted for righteousness' sake,
    For theirs is the kingdom of heaven.
  "Blessed are you when they revile and persecute you, and say all kinds of evil against you falsely for My sake. Rejoice and be exceedingly glad, for great is your reward in heaven, for so they persecuted the prophets who were before you.
Matthew 5:3-12

The cliché "acid test" comes from the times when gold was commonly used in monetary exchanges. The question would often arise as to whether or not the gold coin was genuine. Nitric acid was applied and if the coin was false gold the acid decomposed it, but if it was genuine, the gold coin remained intact. The acid test for Christians is found in the last of the beatitudes. The Bible teaches that those who have been persecuted for the sake of righteousness will have a portion in the kingdom of heaven.

Jesus said to "rejoice" when persecution comes and it will if you are a Christian. There is no way to escape the injunction to rejoice when you are insulted, persecuted, or slandered for the sake of righteousness. The Apostles rejoiced to suffer disgrace for the name of the Lord. The prophets saw the contiguous nature of persecution and righteousness. Study church history, which most churches don't, and you will find numerous martyrs for the sake of Christ. In fact, the apostle Paul said "all who desire to live godly in Christ Jesus will be persecuted" (2 Timothy 3:12). Christian friends, if you have not been persecuted because of righteousness, then review the qualifications for a Christian in the beatitudes.

>   Christians are described as those people who are:
>   1) Poor in spirit
>   2) Mourn after their sin
>   3) Seek after God's righteousness
>   4) Show mercy to others
>   5) Poor in heart
>   6) Seek peace
>   7) Persecuted for the sake of righteousness

The French Revolution introduced a new philosophy for mankind. It was the beginning, in the western world, for the human being to be "a happy man." The war cry of the French Revolution was "liberty, equality, and fraternity." These are expressions of individualism in the full bloom of modernity. Liberty, equality, and fraternity were supposed to be the keys to happiness, but they didn't bring happiness. They brought misery! Happiness does not come from a state of confusion, which is exactly what individualism is, a state of confusion. Do you want to be happy? Read the beatitudes in Matthew chapter five. There you will find the formula for happiness in the Kingdom of God now and the Kingdom of God in the time to come. "0 taste and see that the Lord is good; How blessed [happy] is the man who takes refuge in Him" (Psalm 34:8).

What is a Christian? In biblical categories a Christian is two-dimensional. The first dimension is the state of being. The state of being is concerned about the intrinsic qualities of a Christian. The second dimension is concerned with the activities of a Christian. There is a place in Scripture that integrates both dimensions. It is commonly known as the beatitudes.

A CHRISTIAN IS POOR IN SPIRIT

Jesus said, Blessed are the poor in spirit, for theirs is the kingdom of heaven" (Matthew 5:3). Being "poor in spirit" is a mark of Christian character. Jesus is not speaking of a financial or psychological condition. Christians are poor in spirit when they become aware of their spiritual poverty. A notable example is the prodigal son in Luke 15 when he came to his senses only after he was completely broken. He was emptied of his pride. He was aware of his bankrupt condition. Christians who are conscious of their miserable and helpless condition without the Spirit of God are the Christians who are poor in spirit.

"Poor in spirit" is a state of being; it is not something the Christian does. Poor in spirit is one of several ways to describe the Christian state of being. It will ultimately affect behavior.

Twentieth century evangelical Christianity attempted to abort spiritual poverty by redefining theological concepts and replacing them with psychological theorems. The result is that Christians have become too full of themselves. Self-centeredness is the primary culprit that prevents Christians from being poor in spirit.

What is the reward for being poor in spirit? Eternal life! If we are poor in spirit now, we will be rich in spirit when we dwell in the New Heavens and the New Earth. The Psalmist reminds us that "Yet I am poor and needy; may the Lord think of me. You are my help and my deliverer; O my God, do not delay" (Psalm 40:17).

A CHRISTIAN IS ONE WHO MOURNS

Jesus addressed a crowd of people and said, "Blessed are those who mourn, for they shall be comforted" (Matt. 5:4). His statement precisely describes a Christian. Mourning describes the character of a Christian, not just an activity. You're probably asking the question, why must Christians mourn?

Mourning has become a subject of much talk among psychologists. The primary reason is that mourning is associated with grief. Dr. David Benner, a noted psychologist, says, "Most of what we know about the process of mourning comes from the study of those who grieve the death of a loved one." Any loss, especially death, will effect the emotions, which in turn will affect the entire soul. Benner also says, "Complete emotional healing is impossible [without] mourning.

The beatitudes do not answer the question why; they just explain the necessity and the result. A general understanding of the whole Bible will help us understand why a Christian must mourn.

The psalmist seems to be overwhelmed with his sin and says, "I go mourning all day long" (Psalm 38:6). In the beatitudes Jesus describes a Christian mourning over his own sinfulness. The Holy Spirit convicts us of our sin and then we mourn over our sinfulness. When Christians are conscious of sin, they will be grieved by it.

If it is by God's grace that we mourn, then it is out of God's good pleasure that we are comforted. Yes, we receive comfort from a gracious God who pardons and forgives the Christian. The joy of grief is the comfort we receive from Cod.

Christians find solace in grief just as they find strength in weakness. During the dark period of Israel's history the Lord spoke through the prophet Jeremiah and said, "For I will turn their mourning into joy, and will comfort them, and give them joy for their sorrow" (Jeremiah 31:13).

A CHRISTIAN IS HUMBLE

"We always seem to ourselves righteous and upright and wise and holy -- this pride is innate in all of us unless by clear proofs we stand convinced of our own unrighteousness, foulness, folly, and impurity" (*The Institutes of the Christian Religion*, p. 37). Sometimes we have to define words by explaining what they are not. Humility is not pride. Pride is self-seeking, but humility does not seek its own importance

Jesus described a Christian as one who was meek, gentle, or humble. The Bible teaches that Moses "was a very humble man, more humble than anyone else on the face of the earth." We can learn from that statement that a person who is humble is not a weakling, because Moses was capable of doing hand-to-hand combat. Moses was a rough, tough, and robust man. As a matter of fact Moses killed a man and then spent forty years in the wilderness-tending sheep. No doubt, he became poor in spirit and mourned for his sins. He had to learn to submit to the Lord and to be gentle with sinners.

Jesus is also described as humble and lowly in heart. Jesus humbled Himself and took on the nature of a servant and was certainly submissive to the will of the Father. Christian humility means we resign to God's will and therefore seek the mind of God. A mark of the Christian is humility.

Christians will find security in humility. Jesus said, "Blessed are the meek [humble], for they will inherit the earth" (Matthew 5:5). There is a present dimension to the indicated future promise. Christians can enjoy God's creation now. We can be good stewards of God's blessing in this world by submitting to Him. The future dimension promises an inheritance in the New Heavens and the New Earth for that is the joy of God's benediction upon His people. The Psalmist reminds us that "Good and upright is the Lord. He leads the humble in justice, and He teaches the humble His way" (Psalm 25:9, 10).

CHRISTIANS FIND SATISFACTION IN HOLINESS

Food and water are basic human needs. We hunger for food and thirst for water. Jesus uses these real human needs to describe the Christian state of being. Christians hunger and thirst after righteousness. Perhaps you are thinking "I'm a Christian, but I don't hunger and thirst after righteousness." If you doubt, then think back over your Christian experience. First, you have to be received into the Kingdom of God. Then you become aware of your spiritual poverty, you grieve about your sinfulness, and humble yourself so you will desire the righteousness of God.

In biblical categories, righteousness includes two components. First righteousness must be understood in forensic or legal terms. Righteousness is also requires ethical considerations. First God declares the sinner righteous in His sight. The word "justification" used in relation to the doctrine of salvation in Scripture is always used in a forensic (legal) sense. It is a divine act whereby God declares the elect of God, who are sinners and deserve condemnation, to be acceptable in His sight. The Bible uses forensic (legal) language in the explanation of our standing before God. The Bible also explains righteousness in terms of sanctification and good works. The two cannot be separated. Good works do not make you righteous, but when God declares you righteous, you will do good works (Romans 8:14).

The second dimension of righteousness describes one who conforms to the standard, will, and character of God. A rejection of the second dimension will result in what is known as "carnal" Christianity. This is a rampant and serious error in the church today. Avoid this error at all cost

There is a great blessing for the hungry and thirsty Christian. The intense desire for righteousness will result in a filling by the power of the Holy Spirit. Simply stated, a Christian finds satisfaction in holiness.

The Psalmist discovered that the "Righteousness and justice are the foundation of Thy throne" (Psalm 89:14). As Christians we are all challenged to "seek the kingdom of God and His righteousness" (Matthew 6:35).

MERCY IS A CHRISTIAN TRAIT

The Bible often defines Christians by using general terms like love, goodness, or faithfulness. Even for Christians, the word love can mean several different things. The benedictions recorded in Matthew 5:3-11 describes the nature of a Christian in concrete terms. Christians are people who are aware of their spiritual poverty and grieve about their sinfulness. They also humble themselves before God and desire the righteousness of God. Jesus also teaches us that mercy is a Christian trait. "Blessed are the merciful, for they shall obtain mercy" (Matthew 5:7).

To show mercy indicates one is being moved to compassion. Mercy overcomes the fear of Satan's deceptions. A good illustration is found in Luke 10:30-37. It is the story of the Good Samaritan. It is a good description of mercy, because the Samaritan took responsibility for the sin of someone else. We should be reminded of Jesus who showed mercy to us, because He took responsibility for our sins. If you are a Christian, do you show mercy for the bruised and broken or do you pass by on the other side?

There are many ways to show mercy, but primarily Christians should show the Excellency of the love of Christ in our acts toward other people. However, love is useless without warning about God's justice. The Prophet Micah explains what the Lord requires: "To act justly and love mercy and walk humbly with your God" (Micah 6:8). Justice and mercy are not contradictory, but rather they are complimentary. God's mercy is not capricious for without His mercy, especially demonstrated through the person and work of Jesus Christ, we stand condemned by the guilt of sin.

Christians are not wanting in this grace of mercy. The more Christians abound in mercy, the more Christians will resemble God. No doubt, mercy is one of the hallmarks of a true Christian conversion. The Psalmist assures the Christian that "the Lord will judge His people, and will have compassion on His servants" (Psalm 135:14).

CHRISTIANS ARE PURE IN HEART

"Blessed are the pure in heart, for they shall see God" (Matthew 5:8). To give an honest and full explication of this verse would take a year, but pray for God's blessing to the reading of these brief comments.

It has been said "a thing is pure when it is in harmony with its nature." For instance, water is pure when it contains only the chemical compositions in the exact amounts that constitute water. In other words, a thing is pure when it is unmixed.

The pure in heart are those men, women, boys and girls who are sincere when it comes to belief in the gospel of God. Not only sincerity, but also they must possess the integrity to match the sincerity. Dr. Sinclair Ferguson says, "being pure in heart means letting nothing stand in the way of our vision of Christ." The negative dimension of this beatitude is that an impure heart hinders the soul from seeing God. The positive dimension calls the Christian to a sense of self-awareness under the control of the Spirit of God. Examine yourself to see if you find spiritual poverty, holiness, humility, and mercy. The presence of these characteristics will help you measure your Christian purity.

What did Jesus mean when He said, "the pure in heart shall see God?" This was a major question in medieval Roman Catholic theology. Actually it is a major question to the mind of all Christians, but the evangelical church has been amiss to teach on the subject and therefore people do not know how to frame the question. The way to ask the question is: How does the pure unmixed heart (mind, emotions including our entire psychological makeup, and will) perceive of and delight in the being of God? At the present time you see God through the work of creation, the dispensation of providence, in life's trials, in the sacred page, the means of grace and particularly in the transforming power of God through the Holy Spirit. The time will come when Christians will see God in a new, fresh and full way.

Christians must strive for a pure heart, so they can enjoy the blessings from God, especially to see His glory now and forever. The Psalmist has a word for you spiritual Israelites: "Surely God is good to Israel, To those who are pure in heart" (Psalm 73:1).

CHRISTIANS ARE PEACEMAKERS

The world is filled with peace breakers. History reveals that over the centuries thousands of peace treaties were made and broken. Nations are at war. People are at war with each other and some people are at war with God. Christians on the other hand are peacemakers.

God has graciously made a peace treaty with Christians, which the Apostle Paul describes in his letter to the Romans. "We have peace with God through our Lord Jesus Christ." God initiates the first peace treaty and sets in place the concept known as reconciliation. The nature, person, and work of Jesus Christ are the basis for our peaceful relationship with God and with other Christians.

What is the responsibility for the Christian, since the Christian's nature is to make peace? They are several, but one is particularly ignored in the church today. Christians must seek peace among dissenting Christians. There has been no major attempt this century to reconcile doctrinal differences such as occurred at the Synod of Dort and the Westminster Assembly in the 17th century. We've apparently forgotten or ignored the instructions found in the Bible. "My brothers, if one of you should wander from the truth and someone should bring him back, remember this; whoever turns a sinner from the error of his way will save him from death and cover a multitude of sins" (James 5:19). It is the duty of Christians to endeavor to resolve the problems that separate the visible church since peace making is the nature of Christians.

There is no such thing as "peace at any price." Peace is never brought about by compromise with truth under the guise of love. Even so, in a world of egotism, filled with pride and greed, Christians are makers of peace. The Psalmist has warned us to "Depart from evil, and do good; Seek peace, and pursue it" (Psalm 34:14).

CHRISTIAN IDENTITY IS IN CHRIST

Christians do not have to struggle for identity. The essential characteristics of Christians, truly professing and practicing Christians, are outlined in the beatitudes (Matthew 5:3-11). The

Sermon on the Mount, as it is commonly called, is for God's children and there Jesus gives a definition of a Christian. The Sermon on the Mount is often approached from the ethical dimension. For just a moment, I want consider the indicative dimension of the Beatitudes. That refers to the essence of Christianity rather than the practice of Christianity.

When Jesus announced the "blessings" in Matthew chapter five, He ended them by saying "Blessed are those who have been persecuted for the sake of righteousness. . . ." Persecution comes because natural man hates God. "The wrath of God is being revealed from heaven against all the godlessness and wickedness of men who suppress the truth by their wickedness" (Romans 1:18). Jonathan Edwards said "man is naturally totally ignorant of God in His divine Excellency." Edwards is not saying that natural man is totally ignorant of God, but totally ignorant of the majesty of the divine Excellency of God. Every human has some knowledge of God. Those who have not been born again by the Spirit of God hate what they know about God. Those who have been spiritually re-born by the Spirit of God have a saving knowledge of God's sweetness and Excellency. The Christian is then blessed according to the eight benedictions given by Jesus in the Beatitudes.

A person who has been blessed should become a blessing to others. If you are a Christian, you're like salt and light. Jesus describes what Christians are like in response to a society that hates God and seeks to persecute God's servants. Jesus uses a metaphor to describe the Christian state of being referred to as "like salt and light." If you are like salt and light, then your actions will reflect your state of being. A horse acts like a horse, because a horse is a horse. It is a simple statement, but it is loaded with philosophical and theological profundity. It sounds so simple, let's try another statement. A Christian acts like a Christian because a Christian is a Christian. Jesus explains why in the Gospel of Matthew. Jesus uses two metaphors, salt and light, to describe a Christian.

Jesus said "you are the salt of the earth." We know this is not a literal statement, because a Christian is more than a chemical composition known as sodium chloride. Salt is used in Scripture in a literal sense to flavor and season food, to preserve and cleanse, and to render useless. It is also used as a figure of speech. Jesus uses "salt" as a figure in this text to describe those Christians who act as a preservative in society. Salt not only preserves, it nourishes. Christians serve as a means of spiritual nourishment to a deprived and depraved society. Salt also symbolically serves as an agent to make land unproductive. Christians will make the works of Satan unproductive by teaching and preaching the truth while they pray for reformation. Finally, salt creates thirst. Are you a salty Christian? Do you stand for truth? Most Christians say they believe the truth, but can they defend the truth? I don't know what the statistics are now, but about 15 years ago there were reportedly 60 million evangelical Christians in the United States. If that is true, why is America rapidly becoming one of the most pagan (un-Christian) nations in the western world?

Jesus said "you are the light of the world." He goes on to say you are the light if you "let your light shine before men, that they may see your good deeds. . . ." Natural man is in spiritual darkness, but the person who is born again by the Spirit of God is walking in the light and it must show. Jesus puts it in the form of a command, "Let your light shine before men." Do you hide your righteousness from the unconverted person who desires to persecute you? Do you hide your righteousness from the converted person who might mock your Christian walk? Consider! Children of God should say like the Psalmist, "My heart shall rejoice in Thy salvation" (Psalm 13:5). One way to experience the joy of salvation is to be salt and light in an unsavory and dark world.

Christians are blessed because they do not have to struggle for identity. Their identity is in their source of being, the Lord Jesus Christ. By the grace of God, the love of Christ, and the power of the Holy Spirit, Christians will rejoice that they know who they are and how to live.

Understanding the dignity and majesty of Jesus Christ will help Christians understand their identity in Christ.

There are not enough words to express the dignity of Christ. Webster defines the word dignity in terms of "nobility or elevation of character; worthiness…". It is derived from the Latin word "dignitas". "A word closely connected to the Latin word Gloria is glory, thus the glory of God is the dignity of God." Another Latin word that will help us understand dignity is "gravitas". "The Latin word for importance, esteem and majesty. The English word gravity comes from this and relates to the glory of God" (*Theological Terms in Layman Language*, by Martin Murphy). The following verses from the first chapter of Colossians best reveal and summarize the dignity of Christ.

Vs. 13 – He delivered us from the power of darkness
Vs. 15 – He is the image of the invisible God
Vs. 16 – By Him all things were created
Vs. 17 – He is before all things
Vs. 18 – He is the head of the church
Vs. 19 – In Him all the fullness should dwell

Vs. 20 – Through Him there is reconciliation

We cannot think of the dignity of Christ without thinking of God's eternal purpose, as Paul said, "He chose us in Him before the foundation of the world" (Ephesians 1:4). Therefore the dignity of Christ and our redemption are inseparably related.

It is incumbent upon Christians to understand the dignity of Christ who represents them before a holy God. First, Christ represents His people by saving them from the power of darkness.

Paul said Christ delivered us from the domain of darkness – the unknown. The word delivered means to rescue or set free. Christ saves us from the gloom of eternal punishment and misery. Christ saves us from ignorance and moral blindness. Ask yourself the simple question: Does the power of darkness rule over you? If not, then Jesus Christ has saved you from the power of darkness. I believe you can see how Christ represents His people with great dignity. If your identity is in Christ then you are identified with the supreme dignitary of the universe.

Majesty accompanies the dignity of Jesus Christ. Majesty refers to the imperial nature, stateliness, and sovereign power of the dignity of Christ. The church recognizes the dignity and majesty of Christ. Each member of the family of God is in a unique relationship with the head of the church. The "head" is a figure of speech that denotes the position of Christ in His relationship to the church. As the hymn writer says, "to him all majesty ascribe and crown him Lord of all."

The Lord Jesus Christ provides salvation for His church. Salvation is a demonstration of His supreme majesty and love for His church.

14. Christian Love

A new commandment I give to you, that you love one another; as I have loved you, that you also love one another.
John 13:34

Love is a word often used, but seldom understood. A little girl said to her Mother, "Mommy I love my baby dolls, but they don't love me back." Since love is a generic term, I will use the specific term, Christian love.

Jesus commanded His disciples, which includes all Christians, to love one another. Jesus spoke these words on the same evening that he instituted the Lord's Supper. The Passover celebration changed to celebrate the sacrifice of the true Lamb of God, the Lord Jesus Christ. In the context of this change the Lord said, "I have loved you", which includes all Christians. He demonstrated His love by taking on the form of man, living in this sinful world, suffering death on the cross, then being raised from the dead and ascending into heaven.

Even though Jesus Christ demonstrated His love, it does not define love. The use of the word love at this present time primarily refers to a feeling. It's like eating a good steak; it satisfies the sensual appetite. I believe it is safe to say that love is an emotional response according to many contemporary definitions.

As an emotion, love stands in opposition to hate. Love and hate are basic attitudes of life. God's love is evident throughout

Scripture. "In this is love, not that we loved God, but that He loved us and sent His Son to be the propitiation for our sins" (1 John 4:10). God also hates. "Let none of you think evil in your heart against your neighbor; And do not love a false oath. For all these are things that I hate,' Says the LORD" (Zechariah 8:17). If you have a heavy book handy, throw it on the floor so you will be wide awake before you read the rest of the story. God does hate, but it is different from the hate that comes from a sinful being. God's hatred is holy, because holiness is a primary attribute of God. God's holy hatred is radically different from the sinner's sinful hatred. Since we are incapable of holy hatred, we are wise to remember, "Hatred stirs up dissension, but love covers over all wrongs" (Proverbs 10:12).

Love may express itself through the emotional mechanism that God gave to His rational creatures, but biblically love is an indicative reality that connects the lover and the loved. The lover and the loved have a covenant commitment and the deeper the love the more the commitment. Jesus called this a new commandment because it is based on the new covenant. Jesus, the lover, and His disciples, the loved, have an eternal binding relationship. That is love.

Jesus made love a principle in His life. He demonstrates general love to all of creation because as the second person of the Trinity, he provides for all of creation. He demonstrates his particular love by saving His people. His love exhibits the wisdom found in the full counsel of God. His love is free of prejudice. With His last breath, Jesus prayed for the ones who murdered Him. Sometimes Jesus demonstrates His love by rebuke and correction.

Paul describes love in 1 Cor. 13 as the most excellent way. (See 1 Corinthians 13) Then Paul says the most excellent way (that is love) is defined thus: hopes all things, endures all things and never fails. Did Paul say love never fails! Why would Paul say such a thing? Reading Paul's letter to the Corinthians, it becomes obvious that love was missing, but Paul then said love never fails. In our culture, we define love in these ways: affection, approval, attraction, and so on but they all fail at some point.

Paul says that love never fails and from that, I take his use of the word to mean divine love. The love of God never fails because God's love is perfect. God's love is not utilitarian. God does not love to get something in return for His love. God's love is determined, complete and benevolent. God's love is immeasurable, so we can say that God's love is the highest love. The love sinful people have for one another fails, to a greater or lesser degree.

Jesus gave His disciples a new commandment. We are instructed to love one another as Christ loved us. Why did Christ issue a new commandment? Christ calls it a new commandment, relative to the old commandment that said to "love your neighbor as yourself" (Leviticus 19:18).

The commandment is to love your neighbor as Christ loved you. That elevates your responsibility to a new level in a new manner. We must not only love our neighbor as ourselves, but as Christ has loved us. Jesus repeats the commandment. "This is my commandment, that ye love one another, as I have loved you" (John 15:12). Jesus proved His love with His own blood sacrifice, to the death. "Greater love has no one than this, than to lay down one's life for his friends" (John 15:13). To love as Christ loved requires a sacrifice. If a person does not demonstrate love by sacrifice, it is not loving one another as Christ loves His disciples. In His commentary of John, Dr. William Hendriksen, comments on the new commandment to love one another. "His [Jesus] example of constant (note: keep on loving), self-sacrificing love (think of His incarnation, earthly ministry, death on the cross) must be the pattern for their [disciples] attitude and relation toward one another" (New Testament Commentary, Exposition of the Gospel According to John, Baker Book House, page 253).

There are theological implications connected with brotherly love. The evidence of spiritual regeneration, commonly known as born again, will be brotherly love. "We know that we have passed from death to life because we love our brothers" (1 John 3:14). The word brothers bring the family of God into focus. It is normal for fathers and mothers to love their children and they likewise instruct siblings to love one another. How much more should brothers and sisters in the family of God love each other?

More evidence of brotherly love is found in the doctrine of sanctification. Christians grow in grace and endeavor to turn from sin; the sinner will endeavor to obey God. "If you love Me, keep My commandments" (John 14:15).

All theology turns into practice and the practical dimensions of "love one another" from a theological perspective are many. Love one another begins with a desire for the well-being of another. Self-interest will turn into another's interest.

If Christians love one another justice will become exceedingly important. It has been said that love is the father of justice. You cannot be just to someone you hate, because prejudice will prevail and justice will be curtailed. Justice requires pure and true love. God instructed the Israelites through the prophet Hosea to "observe mercy and justice."

If love is father of justice, then love is the mother of truthfulness. If you really love one another it is impossible to deceive one another. This is especially for those who consider themselves upper echelon of professing Christians. Or to put it another way, self-righteous professing Christians. If the truth is known, every sinner ought to find humility the height of love. Deception overrules truth trumps humility and slaughters the commandment to love one another.

Love comes before mercy. They are relatives in character and practice. God made a covenant to save His people, which was rooted in divine love.

Love is the wellspring of patience. The one another commandment is a preface to all the other one another commandments. "Therefore, as the elect of God, holy and beloved, put on tender mercies, kindness, humility, meekness, longsuffering; bearing with one another, and forgiving one another, if anyone has a complaint against another; even as Christ forgave you, so you also must do. But above all these things put on love, which is the bond of perfection" (Colossians 3:12-14). Patience is a mark of love.

A genuine Christian does not regard God as an abstract concept or an impersonal Absolute. Instead, the believer desires to lead a life that is pleasing to God. Why? Because God first loved us. "In this is love, not that we loved God, but that He loved us and sent His Son to be the propitiation for our sins. Beloved, if God so loved us, we also ought to love one another" (1 John 4:10–11, NASB).

Christians are to love God in response to His love for them, and they are to love each other as a result of their love for God. "We love, because He first loved us. If some one says, 'I love God,' and hates his brother, he is a liar; for the one who does not love his brother whom he has seen, cannot love God whom he has not seen. And this commandment we have from Him, that the one who loves God should love his brother also" (1 John 4:19–21, NASB).

The commandment to love one another must be important. It is often found in the Word of God. The following verses are given for your personal meditation and reflection.

> John 13:34 - New command - love one another
> John 13:35 - Mark of Christianity
> John 15:12 - love each other as Jesus loved
> John 15:17 - This is my command Love each other
> Romans 13:8 - Fulfill the law - love each other
> 1 Thessalonians 3:12 - Overflowing love for each other
> 1 Thessalonians 4:9 - Taught by God to love each other
> 1 Peter 1:22 - Love one another deeply from the heart.
> 1 John 3:11 - Message from the beginning to love one another
> 1 John 3:23 – A command to love one another
> 1 John 4:7 - Evidence of Christianity
> 1 John 4:11 - We ought to love one another
> 1 John 4:12 - Evidence of Christianity
> 2 John 1:5 - challenge to love one another

15. Encouragement is Sweet

Therefore comfort each other and edify one another, just as you also are doing.

1 Thessalonians 5:11

"A word of encouragement during a failure is worth more than an hour of praise after success."

The value of encouragement was so important that Christians are commanded to encourage one another. Dan Clark, speaker and best selling author said, "Encouragement is deciding to make your problem my problem." Then he told the following story.

I would like to share with you a wonderful story I read in *A 2nd Helping of Chicken Soup for the Soul*. The author of the story, Dan Clark, recalls when, as a teenager, he and his father stood in line to buy tickets for the circus. As they waited, they noticed a family immediately in front of them. The parents were holding hands and had eight children in tow, all under the age of 12. Based on their clean, but simple clothing, Clark suspected they didn't have a lot of money. The kids chattered about the exciting things they were expecting to see, and he could tell the circus was going to be a new adventure for them.

As the couple approached the counter, the attendant quoted the price for the entire family. The woman let go of her husband's hand, and her head dropped. The man leaned a little closer and asked, "How much did you say?" The attendant again quoted the price; the man obviously didn't have enough money. He looked crushed. Clark says that his father, who was watching all of this play out, put his hand in his pocket and pulled out a $20 bill and dropped it on the ground. His father then reached down, picked up the bill, tapped the man on the shoulder and said, "Excuse me, sir, this fell out of your pocket." The man knew exactly what was going on, and he looked straight into Clark's father's eyes, took his hand, shook it and, with tears streaming down his cheeks, replied, "Thank you, thank you, sir. This really means a lot to me and my family."

Clark and his father went back to the car and drove home. They didn't have enough money to go to the circus that night. But it didn't matter. It encouraged the whole family. And it was something neither family would ever forget.(www.success-.com/articles/761-encouragement-changes every-thing)

The word encouragement is derived from the Greek word "parakaleo". It comes from two Greek words "para" which may be interpreted "along side of" and kaleo that may be interpreted "to call". God created us with a desire for companionship. It is especially true on the dark days of life. We like to have someone along side us and are comforted by their presence. The Greek word "parakaleo" which may be translated "encouragement" is also translated "comfort" in the New Testament. The comforter may also be our Advocate. "My little children, these things I write to you, so that you may not sin. And if anyone sins, we have an Advocate with the Father, Jesus Christ the righteous" (1 John 2:1). Sometimes the comforter may be our Helper. "But when the Helper comes, whom I shall send to you from the Father, the Spirit of truth who proceeds from the Father, He will testify of Me" (John 15:26).

The Greek religion used the term, parakaleo, during Paul's ministry to beseech healing from the god Asclepius. On one inscription: "And concerning this thing I besought the god." Everyone wants someone to encourage, comfort, and help during the difficult days of life.

The church seems to have forgotten this commandment to encourage one another. The church ought to find delight in this commandment, but she is so busy taking care of her "felt needs" that she is too busy to engage in the noble work of encouraging one another. In *The World According to Mister Rogers*, he left some words that the church ought to seriously ponder. "If you could only sense how important you are to the lives of those you meet; how important you can be to the people you may never even dream of. There is something of yourself that you leave at every meeting with another person."

Larry Crabb said, "People are troubled and restless and angry and desperate and empty and worried. They need to know God and to learn what it means to live in relationship with Him and with His people. Our churches have untapped resources for responding to that need." I believe one of the untapped resources is found in the reciprocal command: 'encourage one another.'"

Jesus Christ did not die in vain. One of the basic principles taught in the New Testament is that we are part of one another within the body of Christ. If we really believe that we are part of the body of Christ, then we stand along side our brothers and sisters in the body with encouragement, comfort, and help.

Christians are in need of encouragement. There is a promise in Scripture that says, "In fact, everyone who wants to live a godly life in Christ Jesus will be persecuted" (2 Timothy 3:12). If the Bible is true and I believe it is Christians are not able to avoid persecution. During times of persecution, Christians need one another. In the season of affliction, encouragement provides strength and motivation to stay on course.

All too often, superficial encouragement replaces Christian encouragement. There was a foreign student visiting a church for the first time. The local people surrounded him with attention and greetings. He was told by several people that they wanted to have him over for a meal and fellowship. He went home and waited on a phone call. No one called. A friend shared a story that reveals the hypocrisy of encouragement. My friend said he visited a church that was known for its theonomic proclivities. In plain language, they believe you must keep the law of God or suffer the consequences. Some of them believe stoning to death is the appropriate punishment for some sins. The preacher waxed eloquent on the subject of hospitality therefore the application of hospitality would be a source of encouragement. After the service, my friend was treated like a stranger with no evidence of hospitality and encouragement. My friend quickly added that he has visited many churches that demonstrated hospitality and encouragement. Hypocrites offer superficial encouragement. Christians offer Christian encouragement.

One of the primary sources for Christians to receive encouragement is from the Word of God. Throughout Scripture, the prophets spoke words of encouragement by the Word of God. The prophet Isaiah is a good example.

> "Comfort, yes, comfort My people!" Says your God. "Speak comfort to Jerusalem, and cry out to her, That her warfare is ended, That her iniquity is pardoned; For she has received from the LORD's hand Double for all her sins." The voice of one crying in the wilderness: "Prepare the way

of the LORD; Make straight in the desert a highway for our God. Every valley shall be exalted And every mountain and hill brought low; The crooked places shall be made straight. And the rough places smooth; The glory of the LORD shall be revealed, And all flesh shall see it together; For the mouth of the LORD has spoken." The voice said, "Cry out!" And he said, "What shall I cry?" "All flesh is grass, And all its loveliness is like the flower of the field. The grass withers, the flower fades, Because the breath of the LORD blows upon it; Surely the people are grass. The grass withers, the flower fades, But the word of our God stands forever" (Isaiah. 40:1-8).

God gives the promise for peace and salvation for the people of Israel during their rebellion against God. The full manifestation of this promise was in the Lord Jesus Christ. God told the prophet to encourage the people because His Word stands forever.

Psalm 119 might be properly titled "Encouragement through the Word of God." "Let Your mercies come also to me, O LORD Your salvation according to Your word" (Psalm 119:41). "Your word is a lamp to my feet and a light to my path" (Psalm 119:105). "The entrance of Your words gives light; It gives understanding to the simple" (Psalm 119:130). These verses remind Christians that God is by their side with eternal words of encouragement.

Encouragement comes in many ways, but Christians are commanded to encourage one another. "Therefore encourage one another and build up one another, just as you also are doing" (1 Thessalonians 5:11, *New American Standard Bible*). Encouraging one another is one of many ways to serve Christ. The writer of Hebrews instructs us to "encourage one another day after day."

(Hebrews 3:13). In this context, encouragement guards against falling into unbelief. Unbelief is the primary goal of false prophets. False prophets produce false belief. Jesus warned the church to beware of false prophets who come in sheep's clothing. The implication is the false prophets may appear to encourage, but all the while they drive a wedge in your faith.

The only way to encourage one another is to be with one another. The writer of Hebrews warns us in these terms: "not forsaking our own assembling together, as is the habit of some, but encouraging one another; and all the more as you see the day drawing near" (Hebrews 10:25).

The elders of the church must possess the gift of encouragement. Elders must hold firmly "the faithful word as he has been taught, that he may be able, by sound doctrine, both to exhort and convict those who contradict" (Titus 1:9). The word exhort comes from the Greek word parakaleo which is also translated encourage. Believers will be discouraged by false doctrine, but they will be encouraged by sound doctrine.

One of the best ways to encourage one another is by teaching one another sound doctrine. In order to teach one another each one must have a summary of the Christian religion. Paul explains that teaching one another requires holding "fast the pattern of sound words which you have heard from me, in faith and love which are in Christ Jesus" (2 Timothy 1:13).

A literal Greek translation of the phrase "hold fast the pattern of sound words" is "have an outline of healthy words."

- The command - have or to hold fast
- Pattern - a summary account - an outline

- Sound words - healthy words - health for the soul

Other than Paul's pastoral letters the word translated "sound words" is only used once by Luke in his gospel in his first letter to Timothy. (See 1 Timothy 1:10). Paul mentions sound doctrine several times. (See 2 Timothy 4:3; Titus 1:9; Titus 2:1).

The only way we can teach one another sound doctrine is by using sound words. The only sound words we have are found in the Word of God. Let me give you a quote from a biblical a notable biblical exegete (John Calvin). "Paul knew how ready men are to depart or fall off from pure doctrine. For this reason he earnestly cautions Timothy not to turn aside from that form of teaching which he had received, and to regulate his manner of teaching by the rule which had been laid down; not that we ought to be very scrupulous about words, but because to misrepresent doctrine, even in the smallest degree, is exceedingly injurious." (Taken from His commentary on 2 Timothy 2:13). Unfortunately worldly passions lead to words of confusion and words of strife rather than sound words. The result is forgotten doctrine and encouraging one another is lost to the passions of the world. Christian friends what we all need is a summary of the sound words from God imprinted on the souls of men, women, boys and girls.

A summary of sound words is not equal to quoting Bible verses. It has often been said that biblical texts may be found to prove almost anything. Unbelievers, the ignorant and scholarly alike use the Bible to prove their opinions. One Bible verse does not equal the full teaching of the Word of God.

When we hold fast to the healthy words of Scripture we will save ourselves and those we teach from doctrinal error. Error in doctrine will almost inevitably lead to error in practice. When a man believes wrongly, he will act wrongly. The very cause of division, schism, quarrels, and bickering in the church is a result of wrong teaching. Christians are not able to teach one another sound doctrine if they ignore the outline of healthy words from Scripture. We cannot hold fast to something unless we understand it. The task is not easy, but it is necessary. Christians are custodians of God's truth and they must hold fast to His truth in faith and love. Then they may encourage one another by teaching one another.

16. Sweet is the Word

Oh, how I love Your law! It is my meditation all the day. You, through Your commandments, make me wiser than my enemies; For they are ever with me. I have more understanding than all my teachers, For Your testimonies are my meditation. I understand more than the ancients, Because I keep Your precepts. I have restrained my feet from every evil way, That I may keep Your word. I have not departed from Your judgments, For You Yourself have taught me. How sweet are Your words to my taste, Sweeter than honey to my mouth! Through Your precepts I get understanding; Therefore I hate every false way.

Psalm 119:97-104

    This Psalm begins with some of the most used words in the English language – "I love". We find it difficult to define the word love. It is one of those words that many people define by expressing what love is like rather than stating in a clear concise definition the meaning of the word love.

    To show you how the English speaking world has grossly misunderstood the word love, I will remind you of the frequently heard romantic expression – "I fell in love." It is grammatically and practically impossible to fall in love. We probably know what people mean, but grammatically it conflicts with the right use of words.

    Love is either a condition or an action relative to the condition. If a condition, an outside force cannot invade it. If love is an action, it could not possibly be passively active. To put it in plain language you can either love or be loved, but you cannot be active and passive at the same time in the same relationship. Plainly stated, it is a contradiction to say "I fell in love."

The 16th century Reformer, Martin Luther, said "The greater the love, the more like God." He went on to explain that the more a person loves, the closer he approaches the image of God." I conclude that Luther intends love to be an expression of affection and a display of selfless service.

Jesus came to serve, not to be served. Jesus showed pity to a wayward world. Jesus became obedient to the point of death. What Jesus did was an expression of His love.

The object of your love is important. In the context of Psalm 119, the object of love for the Psalmist was the word of God. The Psalmist was a lover of the word of God with his whole being. The Psalmist said "I love Your law" that is God's law which is a reference to the entire word of God. The verb love represents an action of the Psalmist. It is Present tense and active voice and as certain as the life of the Psalmist.

The Word of God is an explanation of the source of life. It also explains what God expects from the Christian. The Shorter Catechism gives a brief answer explaining "What the Scriptures principally teach." "The Scriptures principally teach what man is to believe concerning God, and what duty God requires of man." An unbeliever may find the word of God to be disgusting and even repulsive. Maybe if the heart was not too hardened, the word of God could be tolerated, but still hated. But the child of God says, "I love the word of God." In fact, the child of God should have the same attitude as the Psalmist. There should be an inexpressible love for the word of God. The Psalmist loved the word of God to a degree that is unheard of today.

The Psalmist "meditated on the Word of God all day. He was so full of the Word of God that his thoughts were upon the Word of God during the most difficult time. He thought about the Word of God all day long. During the day the Psalmist kept his mind of the word of God even though he was busy working, raising a family, making a living, and struggling against the wicked men around him. At night the Psalmist could rest, but during the day his enemies wanted to kill him. They hated him because he loved the word of God.

We all have trials and troubles in this life making it seem like bitter water. The Word of God may overcome the bitter water with the sweet water of Scripture. If you cherish the Word of God and meditate upon it all during the day, you will find it sweet to your life.

The troubles we face in this life come and go. The Psalmist was not so fortunate. He said my enemies are ever with me. But he derived comfort from the word of God. It doesn't matter where you are on the spiritual growth chart. You may be a new Christian, you may be still drinking milk or you may be eating spiritual t-bones, but wherever you are on the spiritual growth chart, you need sound understanding and true spiritual wisdom

The only place you will find sound understanding and true spiritual wisdom is from the word of God. I say it is sound understanding because the Psalmist said, "Your commandments make me wiser than my enemies." His enemies were not ignorant. Possessing knowledge does not insure wisdom. It is possible to have knowledge without wisdom, but you cannot have wisdom without knowledge.

The Psalmist does not compare his knowledge with that of his enemies, who are obviously unbelievers, but rather he compares his godly wisdom to that of the unbeliever. His enemies were men of human learning.

They may have been experts of the natural world, but they didn't know the God of the natural world. If they do not know the God of nature, they certainly do not understand the wisdom of God's word. In terms of biblical wisdom, the goal of wisdom in this life is to know God.

I have wondered what the Psalmist, writing under inspiration of God, intended to communicate to the church when he said, "I have more understanding than all my teachers." We cannot know for sure, but we must ask the question, "who were his teachers?" The teachers of the covenant community in Israel at that time were the priests and Levites. They should have studied the Law of Moses. In fact, they were in the chair of Moses. However, we know that some of those teachers of Israel neglected the law of God.

They were interested in the tradition of previous generations and formalities of religion. As the Apostle Paul says "a form of godliness but denies the power thereof." Hosea declared, "there is no truth or mercy or knowledge of God in the land"(Hosea 4:1). "My people are destroyed for lack of knowledge. Because you have rejected knowledge" (Hosea 4:6). Those priests (preachers) had understanding, but it was not sound understanding. When they departed from the Word of God their understanding was "every false way.

Too often in the contemporary church preachers and teachers have understanding, but not sound understanding. They do not seek the sound understanding from the full counsel of God. They quote a verse to prove a point.

Let me explain what it means to preach the full counsel of God. It is not just verse-by-verse teaching. The 16th century Reformers referred to the full counsel of God in terms of "sola scriptura" (Scripture alone). Scripture was interpreted by Scripture alone, which saved them from "every false way." The New England Puritans call the full counsel of God "the regulative principle. Same concept as the reformers except they would say Scripture must regulate every belief and every practice in life.

The Bible testifies that the Psalmist had a better understanding of the Word of God than his teachers. One way to help you understand the Word of God is found in this verse, "Your testimonies are my meditation" (Psalm 119:99).

When we meditate we preach to ourselves. We study the word of God and meditate upon it. We inquire into the word of God and meditate upon it. We search the word of God and meditate upon it. For instance, the gospel of Matthew explains that Jesus "will save His people" (Matthew 1:21). Then Paul wrote Timothy and said God "desires all men to be saved." Those verses require serious meditation. "His people" refers to those who will be in heaven with Jesus. Then God is said to "desire" the salvation of all men. Any serious meditation will conclude there is a conflict between these two verses. More meditation is necessary from other parts of the Bible. For instance, meditate on this verse, "God is in heaven; He does whatever He pleases" (Psalm 115:3). Any serious meditation would conclude that God does not "want" for anything. Want means to wish, need, crave, or desire. God is not stressed out because some people are not saved, because God does whatever pleases Him.

The Psalmist had a sound understanding of the word of God even more than the men of old. This must mean that the Word of God gave the Psalmist a better understanding of the tradition and learning. In the postmodern scheme people are taught to love experience and the voices of the present culture. Christian meditation on the Word of God is the better way.

If we are diligent in our spiritual lives we might try to summarize our faith and review it occasionally. One old reliable church creed, the Westminster Confession of Faith, says the Bible was given by inspiration of God, to be the rule of faith and life. It is another way of saying Scripture alone, or regulative principle of Scripture or the full counsel of God. The word of God is our rule, but how often do we meditate on it the way the Psalmist describes his affection for and dedication to the word of God.

The word of God is the instrument God uses to reveal His saving truth. However, the word of God is more than just a book that tells us that we have a happy ending waiting for us at the end of our troubles in this life.

Are you able to say what the Psalmist said, "How sweet are Your words to my taste, Sweeter than honey to my mouth!" The Word of God was not merely sweet, it was sweeter than anything he could imagine. It will be the sweet water to your soul.

About the Author

Pastor James Vickery is a builder and servant of the Lord. He began to pastor God's people at an early age and for years has sought to encourage, edify and build the kingdom of God. Those that know him can attest to his dedication and efforts to grow and bless the work of the Lord. Except for the time he took to further his education, he constantly served as a pastor. Whether he had to work a secular job and pastor or just pastor, he has been faithful to the call he received at a young age.

www.ingramcontent.com/pod-product-compliance
Lightning Source LLC
Chambersburg PA
CBHW071511040426
42444CB00008B/1600